BRINGING YOUR EMPLOYEES INTO THE BUSINESS:

An Employee Ownership Handbook for Small Business

DANIEL BELL

Kent Popular Press

Cover design by Daniel Bell and Cathy Ivancic. Photos by Larry Kelly and John Logue.

This handbook is the fifth in a publication series produced by the Northeast Ohio Employee Ownership Center, Department of Political Science, Kent State University, Kent, Ohio, 44242. The others are:

1. *Buyout! Employee Ownership as an Alternative to Plant Shutdowns: The Ohio Experience,* by John Logue, James B. Quilligan, and Barbara J. Weissmann (1986). Foreword by William Foote Whyte.

2. *Employee Ownership and the States: Legislation, Implementation and Models,* by Catherine Ivancic and John Logue (1986).

3. *The Ohio Buyout Handbook: A 'How to do it' Guide for Workers Becoming Owners,* edited by John Logue (1987).

4. *The Lending Environment for ESOP Companies: The Ohio Bank Study,* by Daniel Bell and Mark Keating (1987).

This handbook as well as publications 1, 2, and 4 are available from Kent Popular Press, P.O. Box 905, Kent, Ohio, 44240.

For copies of *The Ohio Buyout Handbook,* contact the Labor-Management Cooperation Center nearest you.

ISBN 0-933522-18-5 (hard back)
ISBN 0-933522-19-3 (paper back)

TABLE OF CONTENTS

LIST OF TABLES

ACKNOWLEDGEMENTS

Since the early 1970s, Northeast Ohio and other mature industrial regions have undergone systematic disinvestment and job loss. This handbook developed out of an effort to analyze the usefulness of employee ownership as a strategy for retaining and creating jobs. We found that employee ownership offered the possibility of saving more jobs in small business than in any other economic sector. Hence this handbook was written specifically for small business owners. All of the ESOP advantages discussed, however, hold true for large businesses as well.

Large segments of Chapters 1 and 2, and appendices A through E were reprinted from *The Ohio Buyout Handbook*. Earlier drafts of these reflect the efforts of Andy Herrmann, Catherine Ivancic, John Logue, and the National Center for Employee Ownership. The company summaries in Chapters 3 and 7 were made possible by the cooperation of and interviews with Lee Morgan, Antioch Publishing; Glen Webb, Webb Insurance; R.J. McKenna, Bostwick-Braun; Jack Hoye, Fluid Regulators; Rich Biernacki, Fastener Industries; and Steve and Phoebe, Cheeseboard. Cathy Ivancic's preparatory drafts for the piece on Fastener (Chapter 3) and on models of participation (Chapter 8) were highly appreciated. The National Center for Employee Ownership gave permission to reprint "Estate Tax Deduction for Sales to an ESOP" (Chapter 4), excerpts from "Cost Cutter Stores" (Chapter 8), and the "Summary of Legislation on Employee Ownership" (Appendix F). The Midwest Employee Ownership Center gave permission to reprint "Franklin Forge" (Chapter 7). Comments by Dan Haley, Karl Reuther, and Corey Rosen were of great assistance. The preparation of the manuscript is an example of the word processing skills of Mark Keating. The original idea and motivation for the book came from John Logue whose skillful editing kept it within the bounds of academic respectability. This project was funded by the Inter-Institutional Program of the Ohio Urban Universities Program, the Ohio Department of Development, the Cleveland Foundation, and the Gund Foundation. I reserve my deepest gratitude for my wife Pachy, and children, Daniela and Phillip.

Daniel Bell
Kent, Ohio
January 1988

1. INTRODUCTION

- *You are the owner of a family business. Your father built the company from the ground up and you have spent your life developing further what he left you. Although the business has been successful, no one in the family has expressed an interest in running it, and you are approaching retirement. You hate to see years of creation liquidated, yet you have most of your money tied up in the business and want to transfer it to more secure retirement investments. What should you do?*

- *Your business has been doing well for a number of years and you feel that now is the time to expand. Opportunities are available, but you do not have the sufficient capital on hand. The firm is already highly leveraged, and you are concerned about the strain that additional loan service will put on the company's cash flow. The obvious solution is outside equity capital, but you dislike the thought of putting company stock on the market for fear of being exposed to unknown and, perhaps, undesirable investors. What should you do?*

- *You are the employer of a good group of workers who should be with you for many years to come. You are interested in both maintaining a high level of long-term motivation and providing them with future security upon retirement. You feel the company should have a formal plan to reward them for their years of faithful service. What should you do?*

In the last decade, increasing numbers of businessmen and women have responded to these and similar questions with the same answer: employee ownership.

Fifteen years ago the concept of employee ownership was virtually unknown in this country. Employee ownership occurred in distant places like Yugoslavia and was discussed in foreign languages like Swedish. It was not intuitively foreign -- what could be more American than owning the place where you work? -- but it just was not the way business was done.

Today, that has changed. As a consequence of the tax incentives put into place since 1973, 8000 companies employing more than 8 million Americans are at least partially employee owned through Employee Stock Ownership Plans (ESOPs). Though the media have focused on dramatic cases of buyouts to avert shutdowns, in fact, these make up only 1-2% of employee-owned firms. In reality, 19 out of 20 are profitable companies partially acquired by their employees through company contributions to ESOPs, or sold to employees by retiring owners, or bought by employees to avoid other purchasers.

Employee ownership has proved good business. Companies that vest substantial capital in employees outperform conventional companies in the narrow economic sense. A number of studies in the past half dozen years suggest that, when other things are equal, employee-owned companies demonstrate higher rates of productivity growth, sales per employee, profitability, and job creation than conventional firms (see Appendix E).

Employee Ownership and Small Family Business Owners

The growing popularity of employee ownership is due, in part, to its ability to provide new answers to old problems. The media have focused on a few dramatic cases where employee ownership averts a major plant shutdown, saving thousands of jobs. But the majority of the American labor force is employed by small businesses with 20, 100, or 250 employees. Here, too, employee ownership has quietly been saving thousands of jobs.

The backbone of the American economy is the small business. These are the seeds which are constantly planted and collectively produce a growing national wealth. When seen together, small family businesses are a powerful element of the economy; however, as individual units they have often been neglected by the media as well as academics. Unfortunately, little is really known about the breed of men and women who run America's small businesses.

One of the few systematic studies of small business in America was conducted for Chemical Bank by Research & Forecasts, Inc. *Small Business Speaks: The Chemical Bank Report* explores the world of small business owners in New York state. Like most survey-based studies, *The Chemical Bank Report (CBR)* confirms academically what most small businessmen and women suspect. The report describes many of their concerns. Employee ownership can resolve some of these problems, namely, the redistribution of the owner's excessive workload, the amplification of sources of equity capital, and the perpetuation of the business when there is no obvious successor to a retiring owner. The flexibility of employee ownership, which can be partial or 100%, makes it an ideal solution for all three situations.

Owning a small business is hard work. One concern discussed in Chemical Bank's study was the excessive workload that rests on small business owners. The responsibility of running a business on one's own involves a great deal of both stress and time. Often, the owner of a small business has no one he or she can trust to take care of the company while going on a much needed vacation. For many, it is only after retirement that they can sit back and enjoy the fruits of their toil. In fact, 76% of small business owners work nine or more hours a day (CBR table 2.1), and 31% work six or seven days a week (CBR table 2.2). In contrast, 75% would prefer to work no more than 8 hours a day (CBR table 2.3), and 86% would like to devote no more than five days a week to the business. One third of the respondents felt they were sacrificing time with their family frequently, and nearly one half answered that they were sacrificing leisure and vacation time often (CBR table 2.17).

As you would expect, owners of small family businesses are under a lot of stress. Not only is their time for relaxation severely limited, but they also have to shoulder all of the responsibilities of the firm. Some feel that they must be there to unlock the door at 6 a.m. and back again at midnight to close. Since only they know all of the problems facing the company, they often can feel that their employees do not share their concerns. These and many other factors combine to produce a stressful situation. In fact, fully 90% of the owners surveyed experienced stress; 37% were under a great deal of stress (CBR table 2.5). Business-related stress was obviously detrimental. Its adverse consequences included irritability, health problems, difficulty sleeping, difficulties at home, and reduced productivity at work.

The obvious solution is to share responsibility, but it is hard to pay responsible, competent employees enough to hold them and it is often difficult to involve other employees in any responsibility at all. Sharing ownership with employees offers the opportunity to involve them in the business with the same sense of responsibility that an owner has, for that is precisely what they will become.

Finding new equity capital for expansion is not always easy. Finding money to grow was a second concern mentioned in the Chemical Bank study. Unlike large corporations, owners of small businesses do not have an entire department of employees dedicated to financing. When they become aware of an opportunity for growth, they often do not know where to go for equity capital. In fact, fewer than one in four of those surveyed said they were at least somewhat familiar with industrial development bonds (CBR table 4.6). Only one in five were at least somewhat familiar with any other programs of low-rate capital financing (CBR table 4.9).

Employee ownership can bring a flexible low-cost financing resource into the hands of a small business owner. It has been noted for increasing a company's credibility, thereby improving its standing with loan institutions. Employee ownership also allows the business to retain pre-tax earnings as a source of investment capital. These advantages are discussed in Chapter 6.

What will happen to the business when I retire? In contrast to large corporations, small family-owned businesses often depend on one or two people. Not only does the presence of this key figure have a major impact on the actual running of the firm, his or her eventual absence, if not prepared for properly, can shut the company.

While many small businesses are family owned, it is often not the case that other members of the family can be counted on or are expected to continue running the firm after the original owner retires. "Smith & Son" companies are not as common as you might think. When asked the question, "What would you prefer to do with your business when you retire?" (CBR table 2.24), only 5% wanted to keep it in the family. The vast majority of small business owners wanted someone else to continue their business. Only 19% believed their children would want to carry on their business (CBR table 2.27) and only 18% would recommend to their offspring that they go into their business, while almost twice that many would advise entering a profession (CBR table 2.26). While the business was a way of improving one's own situation, most owners want more for their sons and daughters.

Despite the fact that a great number of businesses will not be continued under the management of another family member, the original owners would like to see someone else keep their creation alive. It is only natural that when you spend your life building a company, you would like to have it survive as a part of your legacy. Only 4% of the owners surveyed answered that they would prefer to close their businesses down upon retirement. However, fully 65% said they had not made any preparations for the transfer of management or ownership (CBR table 2.25) despite the fact that the median age group was 51 to 65.

Employee ownership is often the best option for the perpetuation of the small business when no family member wants to continue the business. A sale to a competitor interested principally in the company's market may quickly lead to its liquidation. The case is different when selling the company to the employees which also has advantages for both estate planning and transfer of the owner's interests. Furthermore, over 55% of the entrepreneurs surveyed responded that on-the-job training or work experience is the best preparation for business ownership (CBR table 3.6).

Table 1.1: Employee ownership can help small business owners

- Realize assets with maximum tax benefits

- Plan for transition on retirement

- Raise new equity capital

- Hold key employees

- Increase all employees' involvement in the company

Selling to employees not only makes good sense, it also provides major tax advantages to the seller. The tax on capital gains from sales to employees through an ESOP or coop can be deferred indefinitely, if the seller rolls the profit over into equities of other domestic companies. How this can be done and its advantages are spelled out in Chapter 4.

This handbook examines the several advantages of employee ownership for small business owners and their workers. Employee ownership has been used to solve issues of estate planning, retirement plans, capitalization and more. In the chapters that follow, you will read the stories of several companies which have experienced the benefits of employee ownership: why they chose it and how it has helped their businesses.

2. EMPLOYEE OWNERSHIP

Employee ownership of business is one of the most rapidly growing phenomena in the American economy. Almost unknown a decade ago, there are now approximately 8,000 employee ownership plans employing about 8 million Americans. In about 1200 companies, the majority of the stock is owned by the workers. Most of these are in profitable businesses. Successful, majority employee-owned firms range from smokestack industries like Weirton Steel, Republic Storage and Fastener Industries, to newspapers like *The Milwaukee Journal,* to service companies like Davey Tree and Webb Insurance, to transportation companies like Transcon, to high technology like W.L. Gore and Science Applications.

Worker ownership dates back to the 19th century, when worker-owned enterprises were called producer cooperatives. In the 1830s, workers formed worker cooperatives during strikes and lockouts. Producer cooperatives attained their greatest strength under the sponsorship of the Knights of Labor, the major organizer of labor in the United States before the American Federation of Labor. By 1880, there were over 200 Knights of Labor cooperatives, mostly started through local unions. These included grocery stores, banks, newspapers, and factories.

Some of these cooperatives lasted more than 20 years. Most failed, however, because of lack of capital, overzealous price-cutting, unfavorable relations with business and banks, or lack of confidence by the workers in running their own company. The co-ops that succeeded were often sold by the workers to anyone who could buy shares.

In the 20th century, many examples of worker-ownership have gone largely unnoticed until recently. For instance, there are over a dozen plywood cooperatives in the Northwest which have existed since the 1930s. They were born out of necessity when workers faced unemployment lines if they did not buy the factories from bankrupt employers. In over 30 towns, from Puget Sound to Humboldt Bay, workers started up or reopened plywood mills under worker-ownership and management. These companies, ranging in size from 80 to 450 workers, made up one-eighth of the Douglas Fir plywood industry in 1974.

The Development of Employee Ownership Since 1974

The mushrooming of employee ownership over the last decade is due in large part to the legal recognition of ESOPs in the Employee Retirement Income Security Act of 1974 (ERISA). This act gave statutory definition to a concept introduced by Louis Kelso and Patricia Hetter in *How To Turn Eighty Million Workers Into Capitalists On Borrowed Money* (1967). Kelso and Hetter believed greater economic growth could be achieved by a redistribution of corporate ownership. Since capital is the primary source of an affluent society, "universal capitalism" is a prerequisite for real economic expansion. Corporate ownership had concentrated wealth. A vehicle was needed to redistribute shares of corporate ownership so individuals could gain a viable share of corporate wealth which they in turn could use to develop their personal wealth. As the number of people with multiplying net worth grew, so would the economy at a substantially increased rate. Kelso and Hetter proposed to motivate corporations via tax incentives. Less than a decade later their proposal was made part of U.S. economic policy in the form of ESOPs.

Three Forms of Employee Ownership

The form of employee ownership that is best for one company might not be the best for another. Many factors such as the type of production and the size of the business influence the choice between different forms of ownership.

In the U. S., there are three different legal structures used in employee ownership. Employees can share ownership through conventional stock, buy the firm as a cooperative, or buy a portion or all of the company through an Employee Stock Ownership Plan (ESOP).

Conventional corporations. The conventional corporate structure can be used for establishing employee-owned firms. The employee-owned, conventional corporation is distinguished from other corporations by the simple fact that all (or most) employees own stock and no one but employees own stock in it. A number of early employee-owned firms were established using this structure; they include Vermont Asbestos, and, in Ohio, Republic Hose, Manchester Manufacturers, and St. Mary's Foundry.

The advantage of using the conventional corporate structure without an ESOP today is principally its low cost. Not only are legal fees in setting it up lower, there is no requirement of annual appraisals which raises the cost of maintaining an ESOP. On the other hand, the conventional employee-owned firm lacks the tax advantages of the ESOP, and it will find borrowing more expensive. At the time Vermont Asbestos and Republic Hose were established, ESOPs did not have the advantages they have subsequently acquired.

The historical experience with using individual stock ownership in employee-owned conventional companies suggests that many will eventually be acquired by outside owners. In the case of Vermont Asbestos, many employees sold their stock at a handsome profit, but control passed to outsiders. This could have been avoided by giving the company first right of refusal to shares sold, but the company would presumably not have paid nearly so much. In the case of Republic Hose, the arrangement for the sale of employee stock requires that the outside firm which bought a controlling interest must buy all employee stock at the same price if it buys any, guaranteeing every employee the same deal.

A final, and less easily soluble problem, is that of creating a two-tiered work force in which initial employees are owners but new hires are not. It is very hard to require that a newly hired employee buy shares as the cost of getting a job, and in both Republic Hose and Manchester Manufacturing new hires have typically remained non-owners. In the long run, this will probably erode the motivational advantages of employee ownership. Co-ops and ESOPs typically have mechanisms that automatically convert new hires to owners after a period.

Cooperatives. The cooperative form of ownership has several basic characteristics. Cooperative elements include: democratic control based on one member, one vote; all members have the right to work in the cooperative; and return of profits to owner-members is based on investment of labor rather than capital.

These characteristics make a co-op ownership structure automatically democratic, unlike both conventional corporations and the ESOPs, which can be structured in a variety of ways.

Essentially, a co-op begins when each member buys one voting share. Cooperatives are labor-based firms; thus they limit the allowed rate of return on capital investment. There is no limit, however, on the total return to worker owners. Profits are shared through a "patronage" refund to workers based on the number of hours worked or gross pay. Wages vary according to skill and seniority. The patronage dividend is deductible from corporate taxes.

While Connecticut, Maine, Massachusetts, Michigan, New Hampshire, New York, and Vermont have specific worker cooperative laws, most states do not. Thus co-ops often incorporate under corporation statutes. Most co-ops are small with less than ten employees. Larger producer cooperatives exist primarily in agriculture.

There are thousands of worker-owned cooperatives in the United States. Most are small shops, restaurants or retail outlets, but some are larger firms. Some of the oldest are the plywood cooperatives of the Pacific Northwest.

Employee Stock Ownership Plans. An Employee Stock Ownership Plan (ESOP) is a benefit plan for employees, a financing vehicle with major tax incentives and a means to establish employee ownership.

While there have been modest expansions in the other forms of employee ownership, tax advantages have made Employee Stock Ownership Plans the primary choice. An Employee Stock Ownership Plan (ESOP) is a form of collective employee equity in the company that employs them. Designed to decentralize the ownership of wealth in America, the ESOP uses the tool of tax breaks to encourage companies to give their employees a share in capital formation. What happens is this: the company contributes stock (or cash to buy stock) to the ESOP. ESOPs may also borrow money to buy the stock. The company's contribution to the ESOP (or the repayment of the ESOP's loan) is deductible against corporate taxes; this, in effect, permits tax-free retention of earnings -- but in the hands of employees, not the previous stockholders. While the stock is held collectively in the plan, individual employees acquire vested rights to their shares either immediately or over time; their holdings, which are generally proportional to their wages (though shares can also be allocated equally) first become taxable when cashed in on leaving the company or at retirement. Commercial lenders making loans to ESOPs are permitted to deduct half the interest from their

Table 2.1:   Five major tax breaks for ESOPs

- Contributions of stock or cash, repayment of principal on loans to ESOPs, and dividends paid on ESOP stock are tax deductible.

- Taxes on ESOP shares contributed to employees are deferred until distribution of stock.

- 50% of the interest on loans to ESOPs is deductible from taxable income. The consequence is lower rates for borrowers.

- Owners who sell at least 30% of closely held companies to employees through either an ESOP or a coop can defer taxes provided they roll over the gains into other domestic stock within twelve months.

- Estates can transfer their tax liabilities to ESOPs or coops through providing the ESOP or coop an equivalent amount of stock. Furthermore, estates selling to ESOPs can exclude 50% of the gain from taxable income.

earnings, and special tax breaks for family-owned businesses permit owners to defer capital gains taxes if they sell to their employees through an ESOP or a co-op, provided they roll their capital gains over into stock of other domestic corporations.

ESOPs owe their popularity not only to their tax advantages but also to their flexibility. They can be fitted into existing corporate structures or used to create completely new structures. An ESOP can own anywhere from a fraction of one percent to 100% of the shares. Tax deductible company contributions can vary up to 25% of wages, and can change from year to year. While there are minimum requirements for the pass through of voting rights, ESOP participants usually have little control over the company; in general, ESOPs represent a financial benefit for employees, rather than a source of influence. However, some companies have structured their ESOPs to maximize employee influence and have, in effect, become employee controlled as well as employee owned.

While the 1986 tax legislation reduced or eliminated many widely used corporate tax benefits, the key tax advantages of ESOPs have been retained. Presumably, that will make ESOPs relatively more attractive, although the reduction of the maximum corporate income tax rate from 46% to 34% cuts the value of all deductions. The 1986 law provides an exclusion from estate taxation of 50% of capital gains from sales to ESOPs, and it generally strengthens the position of employees in ESOPs by reducing vesting periods[1] (from ten to seven years), requiring put options for stock bonus plans, clarifying voting rights, and requiring the distribution of ESOP shares to employees on terminating employment for other reasons than retirement or disability.

One in seven companies with ESOPs is majority owned by the employees and this margin continues to narrow as retiring owners sell their firms to their workers. An ESOP differs from a conventional pension plan in two major ways: *the ESOP is designed to invest primarily in the stock of the employees' corporation for the benefit of the employees, and the ESOP is permitted to borrow money to purchase employer stock.*

ESOPs have been the most common financing structure for employee buyouts. In an ESOP buyout, an ESOP trust is established, either in the existing firm or in a newly formed, employee-owned company. The trust normally borrows money to buy controlling interest or 100 percent interest in the new company. This may be done in a single transaction, as usually happens in a conglomerate divestiture, or over a period of years, as is common in the sale of closely held firms. The ESOP trust repays the loan as the company contributes an amount equal to each payment due on the loan into the ESOP trust. In return, shares of ownership are allocated to the workers. It is important to note that in a leveraged ESOP transaction, the buyout is accomplished out of future corporate earnings, not employees' current savings. In many small businesses, conversion to employee ownership occurs when the company contributes cash to the ESOP trust and the trust buys the company stock.

---

[1] Vesting is a process by which an employee acquires the individual right to his or her allocation of stock.

Table 2.2: Pros and cons of different forms of employee ownership

	Advantages	Disadvantages
Conventional	* Inexpensive to establish * No maintenance costs * Flexible	* No tax breaks * Development of two-tiered work force
Co-ops	* Automatically democratic * Some tax breaks	* Some lack of flexibility * Difficult access to conventional borrowing
ESOPs	* Substantial tax breaks to employees and companies * Tax advantaged borrowing * Great flexibility	* Considerable costs to establishment and maintenance

Which is most advantageous? There are advantages and disadvantages to each form of ownership. Co-ops are less expensive legal structures, and they are automatically democratic, but they have less access than ESOPs to traditional financing sources. This is due in part to financial institutions' lack of familiarity with co-ops. Conventional stock ownership is equally inexpensive to establish, but it lacks any tax advantages whatsoever.

ESOPs have important advantages in flexibility and tax benefits. The flexibility of the ESOP structure permits partial employee ownership and transfer to 100 percent employee ownership over time. In the case of co-ops, a one time transfer to 100 percent worker-ownership is usu-

the case. In addition, ESOPs reduce the ESOP firms' taxes because principal and interest paid to the ESOP are tax deductible. This advantageous tax treatment for money raised through an ESOP can make the new employee-owned company better able to operate profitably.

Employees in closely held companies generally receive a "put option" which creates a market for their stock by requiring the ESOP to repurchase stock shares from employees leaving the company. Retiring employees can receive cash for their stock. Since they will presumably be in a lower tax bracket at retirement, their income tax will be lower. An ESOP distribution prior to retirement can also be "rolled over" into an Individual Retirement Account (IRA) to defer taxes or it can be treated, in some cases, according to the IRS rules for income averaging.

3. COMPANIES WITH ESOPS SPEAK OUT

The most popular form of employee ownership from the perspective of the small business owner is the Employee Stock Ownership Plan. The ESOP has been defined and redefined by Congress a number of times since legislation was first passed in 1974. Many businesses have created their own ESOPs at various times since then. The characteristics of each vary according to the year it was introduced and the particular needs of the firm. Some introduced an ESOP to provide a retirement plan for employees. Others saw an ESOP as a solution to estate planning. Still others chose to set up an ESOP in order to transfer their own assets out of the company into other investments. What follows are descriptions of five companies in Ohio: Antioch Publishing, Webb Insurance Agency, Bostwick-Braun, Fluid Regulators, and Fastener Industries. In reading their stories, you will become familiar with the wide variety of uses for ESOPs. You will also be able to benefit from their experiences.

Antioch Publishing Company

The Antioch Bookplate Company was founded in 1926 by Ernest Morgan. Mr. Morgan, a self-avowed Socialist, was an unlikely but successful businessman. At his retirement, he passed the business on to his son in 1970. Lee Morgan took an immediate interest in the welfare of the maturing work force and set the family business on a course which would eventually lead to employee ownership. The company, renamed Antioch Publishing Company in 1981, now employs some 110 people in Yellow Springs and 6 in Fairborn, Ohio, and another 50 in St. Cloud, Minnesota. It also possesses wholly owned subsidiaries in the UK and Canada. Antioch is a leading supplier of book-related sideline items to bookstores. It supplies bookmarks, bookplates, calendars, cards, photo albums, write-on-wipe-off boards, and children's books. Its first Ghostbusters books sold over 2 million copies in 1985.

When Lee Morgan became president in 1971, he felt that the absence of an employee retirement plan was a moral issue. He was particularly concerned for the older employees who were approaching retirement age. Consequently, he experimented with a pension plan. This option was attractive because the plan could discriminate in favor of the older workers on whose behalf the company could make higher contributions. But as government restrictions changed, the pension plan became too expensive. So in 1979, Mr. Morgan chose to set up an Employee Stock Ownership Plan. Now the older employees who participate for 10 years in the ESOP will be receiving at least $25,000 at retirement and the younger ones will be looking forward to over $100,000. Today, the ESOP owns almost half of Antioch Publishing and the Morgan family owns the remaining half.

"The ESOP gave us a double whammy," explains Mr. Morgan. Not only does it prepare employees for retirement, it also provides the company with needed capital. In addition, setting up the ESOP created a market for and put a value on company stock and it kept ownership and control within the company.

Employee interest has grown over the years. "There's nothing like pass-through dividends to drive home the virtue of ESOP stock," he points out. "I am always amazed at how sophisticated people become when their self interest is involved." He believes dividends are the best money the company ever spent because they make the ESOP real. Now the employees ask very complicated questions about their stock and have become accustomed to using many financial terms.

For years, employees have had some input into Antioch Publishing. Since 1946, due to Ernest Morgan's political attitudes, there have been two workers on the Board of Directors, which now also include two from management and five from outside. And at the shop level? "We have informal involvement," states Mr. Morgan. "We're working on a plan to do something similar to quality circles." This will provide a formal structure of participation. Employee motivation has been a key factor in the company's success with the ESOP. "My family does not put pressure on me to make the company grow," explains the president. "I don't care how big we are. I enjoy my work. But the employees put enormous pressure on me to perform." With the ESOP they want to see the company grow and so they are very demanding of management. Specifically, Mr. Morgan believes the ESOP has had a positive impact on manager worker communication, on-the-job performance, product quality, turnover, and worker job satisfaction.

In addition to stimulating employee interest, Antioch's ESOP has generated capital and improved its credit. "We're much stronger with the ESOP," Mr. Morgan comments. "The banks love us." With the ESOP to fall back on, the company was able to borrow in the bond market through industrial revenue bonds (IRBs) at 65% of prime in 1985. Since the IRBs had to be used for capital investments, the more versatile leverage power of the ESOP was reserved for purchasing the owner's stock or acquiring other companies.

Mr. Morgan finds the yearly appraisal required of companies with ESOPs to be an excellent exercise for bringing everyone up to date on where they stand and how they are doing; and they are doing just fine. When Mr. Morgan came to the company as treasurer in 1968, sales were at $353,000, and when he became president the company was actually losing money. When the ESOP was established in 1979, sales were up to almost $3 million with a net profit of $188,906. With the ESOP, Antioch Publishing netted a record $507,521 in 1985 on sales of $10,864,000. With dividends of $3 per share, the average employee received close to $200.

Despite a growth in sales to $14 million last year, the company lost money for the first time since 1971. The loss can be attributed to the costly operation of the bankrupt Holes-Webway Company acquired at the end of 1985 in St. Cloud, Minnesota. Mr. Morgan is confident that the company will turn itself around. He is very excited about buying companies with the increased capital and improved credit of the ESOP. "ESOPs are powerful capital generators." In 1982, the Antioch Publishing Company purchased the Sullivan Printing Works Company, now located in Fairborn, Ohio.

The 50 employees at Holes-Webway will be included into the ESOP in 1987. Although they had a pension plan, the old company had not put money into it for years. "It is pretty crappy and I plan to abolish it," declared Mr. Morgan. "I'm an advocate for ESOPs." He adds, "It [the ESOP] is a very generous benefit." Antioch Publishing's contributions to the ESOP were above 20% of participant's pay consistently in the early years. It dropped to 10% in 1986 due to the loss. The ESOP has 75% of its $2.4 million holdings invested in the company. It has acquired 46% of the company and will be pushing 50% within the next three or four months. Mr. Morgan is considering the sale of his stock to the ESOP when it can afford to buy it.

What advice does Lee Morgan have for other companies interested in ESOPs? "Each company has to look at it separately." The printing industry is capital intensive. The structure of an ESOP would be different with labor intensive businesses. The value of such stock might not hold as much meaning for employees.

Mr. Morgan adds a second consideration. "I get calls every month from companies interested in buying us." Given some cases of corporate buyouts where the courts forced the ESOP trustees to sell stock to outside buyers, it is important to structure the ESOP accordingly. At Antioch Publishing, Mr. Morgan wrote into the ESOP that the trustee did not have the right to sell the stock without the permission of the Board of Directors. Mr. Morgan approves of the new ESOP legislation which requires any decision about selling the stock pass through to the participants. Employees usually vote with management when it comes to avoiding a buyout from an outsider.

Webb Insurance Agency

The Webb Insurance Agency in Lima, Ohio, was founded 80 years ago by Glen Webb. He was joined by his brother Perry when the banks closed in the early 1930s. Though neither is alive today, their offspring have carried on the family business. Glen Webb, Jr., signed on in 1948 and Perry's son Larry joined the company 10 years ago.

Glen Webb, Jr., studied Mechanical Engineering at Purdue University and then went on to graduate from the Harvard Business School. When he joined his father's agency, he found the high turnover rate to be a serious concern. "All we were doing was training our competition," he recalls. The problem was that the employees did not have a piece of the action so Mr. Webb began a profit sharing plan 35 years ago. Since that time there has been no turnover with the exception of deaths and retirements.

Glen Webb recognizes that employee motivation is important for the success of the agency. The motivational advantages of an ESOP made it a natural successor to the profit sharing plan. It was almost like putting a new name on an old concept, so the employees turned over all the assets of the old plan to the ESOP trust.

The Webb Insurance Agency created its ESOP in 1982. As of 1986 the ESOP trust owned 6.25% of the business, and this was predicted to grow to 25% over the next five years. Currently, 10 of the 21 employees participate and the approximate value of their combined holdings is over $1 million. The ESOP invests 90% of its trust funds outside of the business. While the old profit sharing plan was converted over to the ESOP, the employees retain their pension plan.

One aspect of ESOPs which was particularly important for Mr. Webb is that it allows 50% of the inheritance tax to be forgiven. "It solved an estate planning problem for me," he points out. Upon his death, his stock will be sold to the ESOP. While this tax benefit is scheduled to expire at the end of 1991, Mr. Webb is confident that Congress will legislate an extension. He asserts that small family businesses are a key part of the character of America, yet they are disappearing due to inheritance tax. As in the case of the Webb Insurance Agency, an ESOP can be an excellent means of perpetuating these businesses by facilitating the transition from family ownership to employee ownership. Mr. Webb believes that Congress recognizes this. While the 1986 tax reform made some things tougher, it made things better for ESOPs. He concludes, "ESOPs are just going to bloom because of the '86 law."

Mr. Webb also considers the ESOP an ideal device when competing for company contracts. Insurance companies make heavy investments into agencies and are pleased with those which have a means of perpetuating long-term existence. ESOPs provide such a means.

And the ESOP has been good for the growth of the business. The agency now employs 21 people, up from 18. The value of its stock has increased steadily, 13% in 1985 and 11% in 1986. The business acquired a new computer 7 months ago and will be 100% computerized soon. Furthermore, Webb Insurance Agency has bought five other agencies, paying for them out of the added profits. This success can be attributed to strongly improved motivation and productivity. Mr. Webb feels the ESOP has had a positive impact on manager worker communication, on-the-job performance, product quality, turnover, and worker job satisfaction.

The improved motivation is due not only to a share in the ownership, but also a share in the operation of the business. "We were a dictatorship," Mr. Webb explains. "Dad ran this place with an iron hand. You went to him if you wanted a paper clip." But with his background in philosophy and education, Glen Webb, Jr., changed things. Now the Board of Directors is made up of employees and Webb stands for election as president every year. "We're no longer a dictatorship, we're a democracy," he states proudly. "They can throw me out if they want to."

Mr. Webb, who is now approaching retirement, has worked to decentralize decision-making in the agency in an attempt "to raise successors." Jim Shockley is vice-president and manages the sales force. Gary Broughman handles the claims department and property management. Tom Moening is in charge of personnel and has become a self-styled expert on buying insurance agencies. Larry Webb handles the agency's relationships with the insurance companies. Marcia Lammers is in charge of the personal lines department as well as the computer expert. Nevertheless, Mr. Webb admits he is still the chief financial officer; he makes the budget and signs the checks.

With the ESOP, employees recognize that they have a vested interest in the agency's success. When a salesman returns from a meeting, the office staff will ask, "How did *we* do?" Mr. Webb believes the attitude of the people has really improved because they feel "if we succeed, they succeed."

Mr. Webb gives the following advice to other small business owners interested in ESOPs. The three key elements which make it work are management, capital and attitude. It is important to have management in place. He explains that *by turning over a percentage of his stock to the employees, he is counting on them to produce a higher value stock for everyone.*

Capital is also important for the unique situation of an insurance agency. Unlike a factory, there is little machinery and real estate for equity. A leveraged ESOP was not needed since the Webb Insurance Agency found the capital it needed in its profit sharing plan.

The third important factor, according to Mr. Webb, is one of attitude or desire. Everybody has to be sold on the idea. He extends this to his own son who is 35 and considering signing on. "If he did, he's going to earn his own place just like everybody else." While Mr. Webb thinks business people with a more traditional attitude might not be attracted to ESOPs, he believes their acceptance in Congress is because of the fact that they provide a way to perpetuate small, closely held businesses and thus maintain employment. Like many conservative business people, Glen Webb, Sr., came from a poor background and was chiefly interested in making money. Glen

Webb, Jr., admits that he and his employees inherited a good situation from his father, but he concludes, "We took what he gave us and we tripled it."

Bostwick-Braun Company

The Bostwick-Braun Company in Toledo, Ohio, was founded in 1855 by William and Charles B. Roff under the name, W. & C. B. Roff & Company. Oscar Alonzo Bostwick joined the firm in 1862 and became a principal in 1865. Carl Braun was employed in 1866 and was joined in 1868 by his cousin George Braun. They purchased an interest in the company from William Roff upon his retirement. When C. B. Roff retired in 1873, the name was changed to the Bostwick-Braun Company. A century later in 1980, the company made history when it became the first hardware wholesaler to become 100% employee owned. This is significant in an industry where businesses face ever increasing odds in the struggle for survival.

Prior to 1980, Bostwick-Braun was a closely-held company controlled by its chairman, H. L. Thompson, Jr. Since his children had chosen careers outside of the business, Mr. Thompson wanted to find a way of perpetuating his company which would be an alternative to selling to a larger company. In order to prevent this or, even worse, purchase by a liquidator, the company began to explore the possibility of an ESOP.

The sale of the company to its employees took a unique form. First the old company changed its name to Bostwick Investment Co. Then, nine company officers formed a "new" Bostwick-Braun Co., contributing $5000 each to purchase stock. This $45,000 was used as a down payment on the company with $60 million in sales. The rest of the debt was from the "new" company to the original owners, who agreed to take a subordinate debt position. Next, an ESOP was formed. The assets of Bostwick-Braun's profit sharing plan were transferred to the ESOP which purchased newly-issued stock. This cash was used to make the first payment on the debt. Subsequently, the company has made regular cash contributions to the ESOP (taking the tax deduction), which the ESOP uses to buy more stock; the cash then is used to continue paying down the note.

As of 1986, 210 of Bostwick-Braun's 300 employees participated in the ESOP worth $2.5 million. Due to the unique set-up of the purchase, the ESOP immediately owned 99% of the company, the remainder belonging to the nine company officers. The company has structured its ESOP to be able to pay off its debt as soon as possible. It has adopted a slow vesting schedule and 5-year installment buy-back program on distributed stock to slow down the cash drain to outgoing employees. It has also combined a stock bonus plan with a money purchase plan in order to increase the amount it can deduct for contributions to the ESOP from 15% to 25% of covered payroll.

The Money Purchase Stock Ownership Pension program is a fixed contribution plan which receives 10% of payroll each year. The flexible contribution to the ESOP can add up to 15% more. For instance, if total earnings make possible a contribution of 22% of payroll, 10% would go into the fixed contribution and 12% into the ESOP.

An outside consulting firm appraises the stock and establishes its fair market value annually. This information is passed on to the employees, along with the number of shares they have. Each employee sees that when the company is profitable, the value of his or her assets goes up by the increased value of each share in addition to the current year's allocation to his or her account. The number of shares times the share value gives the total dollar value of the employee's account.

While Bostwick-Braun has not devised a plan to distribute dividends to its employees, it is planning other modifications which will provide benefits, such as allowing employees to borrow against their ESOP accounts. The company magazine also proudly displays "An employee owned company" as part of its logo. This increased awareness of the fruits of ownership is designed to maintain employee interest in the company's success. This is important since the employees do not have a formal structure of participation in the firm's management to deepen their identification with their company. "They (the employees) can't negotiate with banks and suppliers," points out R. J. McKenna, personnel manager. "They have their own jobs and they have to relegate general management to somebody else. Still, the employees like to feel they have a voice." For example, the employees had a hand in the selection process of the company's new central warehouse site in Ashley, Indiana.

Mr. McKenna says that there has been a definite increase in communication since the establishment of the ESOP, and that employees are better informed in general. Nevertheless, he believes there has not been a significant change in management employee relations since "we have good relations with our employees anyhow." Mr. McKenna recognizes that the key factor in setting up the Bost-wick-Braun ESOP was as an alternative method of owner-ship to a merger or liquidation. The ESOP provided a market for the type of business which is not readily sala-ble. Given this intention, he advises other companies in-terested in ESOPs, "Don't expect too much." An ESOP alone, without accompanying structures of participation cannot be expected to produce revolutionary advances in employee motivation. Nevertheless, "Be prepared to com-municate with the employees," he counsels.

The Bostwick-Braun Co. is a fine example of how an ESOP can be used creatively to provide a way out for a retiring business owner. The company has continued to perform profitably under employee ownership. Mr. McKenna concludes, "It should make a nice living for all the employees, as well as secure a nest egg for the fu-ture."

Fluid Regulators Corporation

Fluid Regulators in Painesville, Ohio, was founded in 1953 as an offshoot of Fluid Controls. It designed valves to be applied in aircraft which requires controls of far greater technical precision than standard commercial con-trols. Before the creation of its ESOP in 1982, the company was owned by four managers: Jack Hoye, president; Warren Cave, vice-president of manufacturing; Mike Cencula, vice-president of engineering; and Malcolm Cro-foot of quality control.

Mr. Hoye created Fluid Regulators' ESOP in 1982. He was in his late 50s and beginning to think about re-tirement. "I want to get out when I retire," explains Mr. Hoye. He was attracted to an ESOP because it could create a market for his and the other owners' stock. When he retires he will sell his stock to the ESOP and will be able to roll-over his money into another investment without paying any taxes on his capital gains.

Two other partners have already taken advantage of this procedure. When Mr. Cave left the company, his stock was bought by the ESOP. The ESOP was able to obtain a low-cost loan from a bank which had been influenced by the tax break associated with such loans. Banks are only taxed on 50% of the interest they earn from loans to ESOPs. Mr. Crofoot subsequently sold his stock to the ESOP.

Over the last five years, Fluid Regulator's employees have acquired 1300 shares or one third of the company.

At over $2000 a share, the ESOP trust is worth more than $2.6 million; 85% of this is invested in the business. As of 1986, all 105 employees were participating in the plan.

Fluid Regulators has been quite successful since the creation of the stock plan. The company grew from 70 employees in 1981 to 105 in 1986. The value of its stock has grown considerably higher than the industry average, 26% in 1985 and 30% in 1986. Have the employees been motivated by the ESOP? "It's just starting now," says Mr. Hoye. "It's taken about four years." Some retirees have walked away with $15,000 to $20,000 which is something they would not have had. Younger employees now have $20,000 to $30,000 in the ESOP. "It's tough to get excited about something they're not going to get until they're 65," observes Mr. Hoye. Nevertheless, he believes that the ESOP has had a positive impact on absenteeism, manager worker communication, on-the-job performance, product quality, turnover, and worker job satisfaction.

Employee benefits from the ESOP include a nominal annual dividend, company contributions, and substantial retirement security. But the principal motivator, says Mr. Hoye, "is the appreciation of the stock. Last year it went from $1640 to $2065 per share." For the average employee who owns twelve shares, that was $5,100 in additional assets.

Fluid Regulators has not instituted a formal structure of employee participation, but it does have monthly meetings where financial information is provided. The workers also have the right to vote their stock in the case that the company were to be sold. While they are presently in the minority, the ESOP trust will own a majority of the company when Mr. Hoye retires and sells his stock to it.

Mr. Hoye does not attribute his company's success completely to the ESOP. For the ESOP to be successful, the business should be successful and growing. "I think it's a good situation, especially for a small privately owned company," he states. "Most small companies don't have pension plans because they cannot afford them." Prior to its ESOP, Fluid Regulators made no provision for employee retirement. Now, the employees see this retirement plan as well as the ability to buy out the owner as a great incentive. Is the improved productivity at Fluid Regulators a result of this incentive? Mr. Hoye is not ready to claim that, but he points out, "every year (since the ESOP), we've increased sales and reduced our cost of sales."

Fastener Industries

Fastener Industries in Berea, Ohio produces a product that most of us come in contact with almost everyday. The company manufactures weld fasteners. These are the nuts and screws that hold metal machinery and equipment together. Frying pans, automobiles, file cabinets, refrigerators, and computers are all held together by the specialized nuts and screws made at Fastener. In a time when basic industry in the United States is struggling, Fastener Industries stands out as a success story.

Originally incorporated as the Ohio Nut and Bolt Company, the firm was founded in 1905. The R. J. Whelan family purchased controlling shares in the 1930s and ran the company for more than fifty years.

Not only was Fastener consistently profitable for the Whelans, it also offered its employees a good place to work. Workers earned above average wages, bonuses, and benefits while those in production worked only a 35 hour week. They were also compensated by a profit sharing plan.

Rodrick Whelan Jr. decided to sell the business and retire in 1979. He did not have to look far to find a buyer for the successful company. At the suggestion of Richard Biernacki, then Treasurer (now President), the company was sold to the employees through an ESOP. "After all, it was the productivity of the employees that was responsible for our profits. By sharing ownership democratically, I figured the company could improve on its already successful track record. And in fact, it has," says Mr. Biernacki.

Fastener's 125 employees had the opportunity to transfer part or all of the money in their profit-sharing accounts to an ESOP. Eighty-five percent of the profit-sharing capital was invested. With the addition of supplemental bank loans, Fastener Industries became 100% employee-owned in 1980. All of the company stock is held in the ESOP.

The plan at Fastener has been cited as a "model ESOP." The company contributes 15.5% of payroll to the ESOP annually, the most allowable by law for a non-leveraged ESOP. As a consequence, the value of the ESOP holdings have grown to approximately $9,600,000, after only six years. Retiring and terminated employees have cashed in their ESOP stock for an average of $100,000 to $110,000.

But financial success is only one reason why many people see Fastener as a model ESOP company. The National Center for Employee Ownership notes that at Fastener, "Ownership culture is a prevailing force." Workers may participate in the plan after only one month of employment. While most firms have gradual vesting schedules, employee owners at Fastener are immediately vested. "One of the worst things that can happen is to have an employee who really doesn't want to work for the company but stays around to become vested," explains Biernacki.

Employee owners have full voting rights on the stock. Candidates for the Board of Directors are nominated directly. Anybody in the company can run. Then the employees vote their shares, one share one vote. Since Biernacki, the major stockholder, only owns 4% of the stock, there is a real equality among voters. After the last biennial election, positions on the Board were won by the president, two plant managers, a machine operator and a warehouse employee. Once elected, the Board takes a very active role in running the firm. Any capital expenditure above $10,000 is subject to Board approval.

Employee owners are kept up to date on company matters in several different ways. Each employee receives the company's annual financial report as well as interim reports throughout the year. Twice a year Biernacki holds a series of roundtable discussions with employees to hear their concerns and share information. Each roundtable is limited to about twelve employees, so there is ample opportunity for give and take in these meetings. Each worker has the opportunity to participate in two roundtables annually. In addition to these formal structures of participation, employees often meet with managers and officers informally.

The ESOP at Fastener Industries seems to have benefited all the interested parties. It provided the Whelan family with a way to transfer its assets out of the company. It gave employees the opportunity to become owners of a successful and viable business. Biernacki personally believes so strongly in the importance of employee ownership to the success of the company that he asserts, "Our company would set up a plan even if there were no tax benefits." That view is mirrored by employees. As Paul Lake, Traffic Manager at Fastener, puts it, "We're all in this together and we're all accountable to each other."

4. ESOPS PROVIDE A WAY OUT

ESOPs and Departing Owners

Many business owners have dedicated their life to building up a successful company. As long as they were running the store, they were able to gain their livelihood from their lifetime investment. But when they approach the age of retirement, they know that the capital they have tied up in their business will serve their interests better in other more diversified investments. Most owners have two expectations at this point. One is to transfer the maximum capital from their business to other investments which enable them to live in the manner to which they have become accustomed, including proper medical care for them and their spouse throughout retirement. The other is to ensure that their lifetime creation continues long after their departure.

There are a number of obstacles to achieving these two goals simultaneously. In order for you, as a small business owner, to turn your investment into cash, you must find a market for your stock. Second, in order to hold on to as much of that cash as possible, you must find a way to shelter it from taxation. Now that capital gains are treated as part of regular income, the sale of your stock can easily put you into the top tax bracket. You can lose quite a large chunk of potential investment capital for retirement earnings. Assume the cost basis of your business were $500,000 and you were to sell it for $1 million. You would have to pay the federal government $140,000; that capital if invested at 10% return could increase your yearly retirement income by $14,000 (see table 4.1).

Two decades ago, the most popular means of deferring this kind of tax was a stock swap with a corporation. A business owner could swap stock in his or her company for stock of equal value in a larger corporation. However there are several drawbacks to this plan. First, you must swap at least 80% of your stock with the same corporation. So much for a diversified investment portfolio at retire-

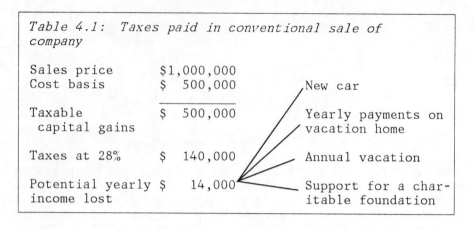

Table 4.1: Taxes paid in conventional sale of
company

Sales price	$1,000,000	
Cost basis	$ 500,000	New car
Taxable capital gains	$ 500,000	Yearly payments on vacation home
Taxes at 28%	$ 140,000	Annual vacation
Potential yearly income lost	$ 14,000	Support for a charitable foundation

ment. Not only will all your money be tied up in one place,
there is also no flexibility in the way you withdraw from
your business. You cannot sell smaller portions over a
gradual period of withdrawal; rather you must make a
major break all at once.

Selling to a large corporation has another drawback
regarding the second goal of seeing your lifetime work
continue. Usually, when a large corporation buys a small
company, it does so in order to acquire its customers,
trademarks or assets. Frequently, it is simply an opportunity to eliminate a competitor from the market. There
is little guarantee that your company will continue to operate or that your employees will keep their jobs.

All of these considerations are based on the assump-
tion that you can find a buyer. Many businesses, while
producing a livelihood for their owners and employees, hold
little attraction as an investment for someone else. It is
for this reason, as well as those previously mentioned, that
companies like Bostwick-Braun have turned to Employee
Stock Ownership Plans.

The former owners of Bostwick-Braun devised an in-
teresting, if uniquely complicated plan for transferring
ownership of their company to the employees and gradually
withdrawing their capital. The plan is illustrated in table
4.2. While this plan is rather atypical, it did solve a
number of problems for the transfer of the company.
First, it created a market for the sale of a company in what
Hardware Retailing Magazine terms "an industry where
businesses of that type face ever mounting odds in the
struggle for perpetuation." Second, while the previous
owners began with all of their capital invested in the

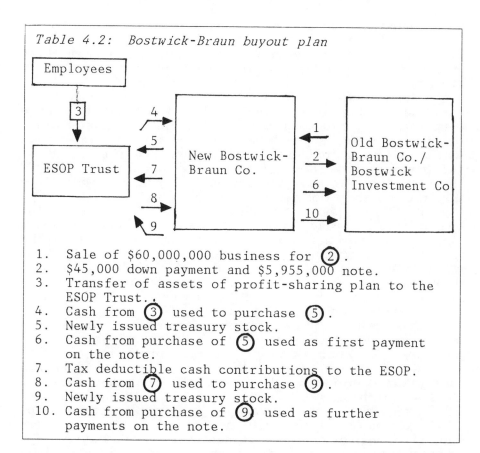

Table 4.2: *Bostwick-Braun buyout plan*

1. Sale of $60,000,000 business for ②.
2. $45,000 down payment and $5,955,000 note.
3. Transfer of assets of profit-sharing plan to the ESOP Trust.
4. Cash from ③ used to purchase ⑤.
5. Newly issued treasury stock.
6. Cash from purchase of ⑤ used as first payment on the note.
7. Tax deductible cash contributions to the ESOP.
8. Cash from ⑦ used to purchase ⑨.
9. Newly issued treasury stock.
10. Cash from purchase of ⑨ used as further payments on the note.

company, they were gradually able to withdraw it in the form of payments on the note in order to reinvest it elsewhere.

The ESOP was useful for reducing the impact of such a heavy debt on the company's cash flow. Bostwick-Braun could use pre-tax profits to make payments on the note by making tax deductible contributions to the ESOP which were immediately reinvested into the company.

Bostwick-Braun's owners sold their business before the tax law had been changed making such complicated systems of transfer unnecessary. Today, most owners would be better off to sell their stock directly to the ESOP because the capital gains from such a sale can be rolled over into other American corporate securities (including stocks and bonds), deferring taxes until those securities are sold. In order to qualify for this tax deferment, the owner must sell to an ESOP or co-op which will control at least 30% of the stock at the end of the transaction. The purchase of other securities can take place from three months prior to fifteen months after the sale of stock to the ESOP.

The flexibility provided here is a powerful advantage over the previous procedure of selling a lump 80% to a large corporation. As demonstrated by the Fluid Regulators case described above, separate members of a partnership can withdraw from a business at the convenience of each. While two partners have already sold their stock to the ESOP, the remaining two have the security of a guaranteed future buyer when they decide the time is right.

In this respect, the ESOP is not only useful to the owner who is ready for retirement. It also provides younger entrepreneurs with greater access to the capital invested in their business should they need cash for some other investment. As long as the ESOP holds a minimum of 30% of the company stock, the owner can sell any amount of stock to it which is convenient at the time, and reinvest the proceeds without paying taxes.

The cash required for the purchase of an owner's stock can come from a variety of sources. Sometimes a company like Webb Insurance Agency or Fastener Industries will have a preexisting profit sharing plan which can be converted into an ESOP. The ESOP trust then uses this cash to purchase stock from the owner. Another way the ESOP acquires cash is from tax deductible contributions of the company out of yearly profits. If neither of these methods can provide the sufficient cash needed at the time of purchase, the ESOP can borrow money from a bank as was the case at Fluid Regulators with the purchase of stock from its vice-president of manufacturing. Banks are generally willing to make such loans at a low cost, because they receive additional tax advantages, too. These advantages are discussed in Chapter 6. In effect, the ESOP repays the loan with tax deductible cash contributions from future profits. An ESOP which takes out such a loan is call a leveraged ESOP.

The Advantages of an ESOP for Estate Planning

In the past, the death of an owner or a major partner in a business has had the potential of causing catastrophic damage to the company. Many businesses were forced into sale or liquidation in order to provide cash to pay estate taxes. Congress recognized the devastating effect this has on employment and the economy and chose to do something in order to avoid these unnecessary liquidations of viable family businesses. ESOP legislation in 1984 and 1986 provided a way to ensure the perpetuation of small companies despite the decease of an owner or major partner.

"It solved an estate planning problem for me," says Glen Webb of the Webb Insurance Agency. Congress has legislated that, until 1992, 50% of the proceeds of the sale of stock to an ESOP by an estate prior to the filing date for the estate tax may constitute a deduction from the decedent's gross estate. This can be quite a tax savings (see table 4.3).

Table 4.3: Estate tax savings achieved with an ESOP

Estate without ESOP		Estate with ESOP	
Taxable estate other than company stock	$ 100,000	Taxable estate other than company stock	$ 100,000
Company stock	$1,500,000	Proceeds from sale of stock to ESOP	$ 1,500,000
Taxable estate	$ 1,600,000	Taxable estate	$ 850,000
Non-taxable	$ 0	Non-taxable	$ 750,000
Tax at 38%	($ 608,000)	Tax at 28%	($ 238,000)
Estate after taxes	$ 992,000	Estate after taxes	$ 1,362,000

Tax savings by the estate selling to
the ESOP = $370,000
Tax rates used are approximations. Actual rates vary
from 18% to 50%.

Table 4.4: Sharing the estate tax savings	
Estate without ESOP	Estate with ESOP
Taxable estate other than company stock $ 100,000	Taxable estate other than company stock $ 100,000
Company stock $1,500,000	Proceeds from sale of stock to ESOP at 13% discount $1,305,000
Taxable estate $1,600,000	Taxable estate $ 752,500
Non-taxable $ 0	Non-taxable $ 652,500
Tax at 38% ($ 608,000)	Tax at 28% ($ 210,700)
Estate after taxes $ 992,000	Estate after taxes $1,194,300

Discount in stock purchase price to ESOP = $195,000
Tax savings by the estate selling to
  the ESOP = $202,300
Tax rates used are approximations. Actual rates
  vary from 18% to 50%.

Of course, in practice the trustees for the ESOP will negotiate for a discount in the stock purchase price and would accordingly receive a share of the estate tax savings (see table 4.4).

Estate Tax Deduction For Sales to an ESOP[2]

"In order to encourage a decedent's estate to sell shares of employer stock to an ESOP or an eligible worker-owned cooperative, the Tax Reform Act of 1986 added Section 2057 to the Internal Revenue Code to provide that 50% of the proceeds from such a sale will constitute a deduction from the decedent's gross estate for federal estate tax purposes. This provision is effective for sales after October 22, 1986, and prior to January 1, 1992, in cases where the federal estate tax return is due (including any extensions) after October 22, 1986.

"In the case of a closely-held company, the shares sold to the ESOP must be either voting common stock or preferred stock that is convertible into voting common stock. In the case of a publicly-traded company, the shares must be publicly-traded common stock (voting or non-voting) or convertible preferred stock. The shares must not have been acquired by the decedent (or, presumably, his estate) in a distribution from a qualified employee benefit plan or through the exercise of a compensatory stock option. There is no requirement that the decedent must have been an employee, officer, director, or founder of the employer maintaining the ESOP. There is also no requirement that the ESOP own a minimum percentage of the stock for a minimum period of time following the sale.

"The shares acquired by the ESOP may not be allocated to the ESOP accounts of the decedent, certain of his relatives (although 5% of the shares may be allocated to his lineal descendants) or any 25% shareholder of the employer. In addition, other assets of the ESOP (or amounts under another qualified employee plan) may not be allocated to those individuals to 'make up' for the prohibited share allocation. If this allocation prohibition is violated, those individuals will be currently taxed on the amounts allocated to them (whether they are vested or non-vested) and the employer must pay an excise tax equal to 50% of the amount involved.

---

[2] This section was written by Ronald L. Ludwig and Anna Jeans of Ludwig & Curtis and is reprinted by permission from the National Center for Employee Ownership.

"In order for the estate tax deduction to be allowed, the executor of the estate must sell the shares to the ESOP (and receive the sale proceeds) prior to the due date (including extensions) for filing the federal estate tax return. The executor must file with the IRS a written statement of the employer (sponsoring the ESOP) consenting to the application of the 50% excise tax which applies to prohibited allocations under the ESOP.

"Since an ESOP is in a unique position to generate estate tax savings for the decedent's estate, the ESOP has the power and the obligation to bargain with the estate for purchase of the employer stock at a discounted price. The ESOP thus would receive a portion of the estate tax savings through a bargain purchase (below current fair market value). It appears that the discount to the ESOP should be at least 10%.

"A significant controversy has arisen over the ESOP estate tax deduction since it became effective last October. It appears from various floor statements of former Senator Russell B. Long that the provision was intended to be limited to stock which was owned by the decedent prior to death. The statutory language of Section 2057 and the underlying Committee reports do not make this intent clear. Accordingly, many advisers have recommended to executors of estates that they acquire stock (after the death of the decedent) for sale to an ESOP. In addition, it appears that certain ESOPs have been advised that they can sell existing holdings of employer stock at the time they acquire 'discounted' stock from an estate. If these practices were to be permitted, the revenue loss caused by the ESOP estate tax deduction would be far greater than estimated at the time the provision was proposed by Senator Long.

"On January 5, 1987, the IRS released Notice 87-13 to provide guidance on certain employee plan provisions of the Tax Reform Act. With respect to Section 2057, IRS has attempted to close the 'loopholes' referred to above by requiring the following conditions to be satisfied in connection with the estate tax deduction:

(1) the decedent must have directly owned the employer securities immediately before death; and

(2) the employer stock must be held by the ESOP for allocation to participants' accounts and may not be substituted for stock previously owned by the ESOP.

"It is clear that this matter will be addressed by Congress in 'technical corrections' legislation in the near future. At a public hearing on February 4, 1987 Senate Finance Committee Chairman Lloyd Bentsen stated that corrective action would be taken (apparently House Ways and Means Committee Chairman Dan Rostenkowski agrees) and likely would be applied retroactively.

"It is unfortunate that the noble goal of broadened stock ownership through ESOP tax incentives promoted by Senator Long over a 13 year period has been tarnished by certain estate and tax advisors seeking loopholes in the Internal Revenue Code. Prompt action by Congress to clarify the original intent of the ESOP estate tax deduction and to provide appropriate limits and safeguards should be encouraged by all ESOP supporters."

Financing the Purchase of Stock from an Estate

The ESOP trust can purchase the stock with cash acquired in any of the ways mentioned above in the section *ESOPs and departing owners.* Employees can also use the federal government to finance their purchase of company stock by assuming part or all of an estate's liability for federal estate taxes. In return for this, the estate transfers company stock to the ESOP with a value up to the assessed estate tax. If the value of this stock exceeds 35% of the adjusted gross estate, the company can guarantee the payment in installments over a period of up to 14 years via contributions to the ESOP.

Thanks to the favorable tax legislation regarding ESOPs, thousands of small family business owners nearing retirement are now able to take capital out of their businesses while minimizing taxes and insuring that their companies can continue to operate independently and successfully, providing continued employment and security for those very employees who have helped to make the business what it is.

5. ESOPS ENHANCE YOUR EMPLOYEES' FUTURE

The most important element of any business is the skill and dedication of its employees. Without a good, stable work force, a company cannot expect to compete. Small, family-owned businesses are at a disadvantage when it comes to retaining employees. Employees often choose to go to larger corporations which can offer an attractive benefit package: pension plan, medical benefits, dental insurance. "All we were doing was training our competition," observed Glen Webb of Webb Insurance Agency.

The Employee Stock Ownership Plan provides the smaller company with the means to offer its own benefit package to its employees. Workers who would otherwise have little incentive besides a wage to stay with a firm can, with an ESOP, look forward to long-term rewards like a retirement plan and job security. Employers can also use the ESOP for immediate motivation in the form of dividends and participation.

The ESOP as a Retirement Plan

While no one responsible for the welfare of a group of workers would recommend to them that they discard a good pension plan for an ESOP, some companies have created ESOPs in addition to their pension plans. Others, without pension plans, have created ESOPs to fill that gap. As Jack Hoye of Fluid Regulators says, "Most small companies don't have pension plans because they cannot afford them." Fluid Regulators introduced an ESOP to meet this need.

Lee Morgan of Antioch Publishing Company felt the absence of a retirement plan at his company was a moral issue. He created an ESOP plan for his employees in 1979. Now older employees who participate in the plan for ten years will retire with at least $25,000 in assets which they otherwise would not have. Both companies, as well as the others mentioned in this handbook, see the value of an ESOP for the employees of small family-owned businesses.

Workers who could previously look forward to little more than social security and a gold watch when they retired, can now expect to walk away with a lump sum of $5,000, $30,000, or $150,000 depending on their years of service.

The value of an ESOP as a retirement plan depends on three factors: the annual company tax-deductible contribution to the ESOP, how that contribution is allocated to employees in stock, and the appreciation of that ESOP stock. A 1985 study by Jonathan Feldman and Corey Rosen[3] examined the average appreciation of ESOP stock and the average percentage of payroll that companies contributed to ESOPs. The study found an average appreciation of 12% a year and an average contribution of 9% of payroll annually. Using these figures, Feldman and Rosen determined that an employee who earned the national median income of $18,000 a year could expect to own ESOP stock with a value of $29,000 after 10 years, $120,000 after 20 years, and $400,000 after 30 years. Feldman and Rosen recognized that these figures were higher than what one might expect because the averages included some firms with phenomenal and presumably unsustainable rates of growth. In order to capture a sense of what the typical firm could expect, they also looked at the appreciation and contribution of firms in the normal range. Using the median instead of the average, they came up with a stock appreciation of 7.5% and an annual contribution at 8.4% of payroll. Using these figures, the same employee could expect about $21,000 in 10 years, $65,000 in 20 years, and $157,000 in 30 years. Considering the fact that many workers who earn a similar salary have accumulated very little capital when they retire, these sums are quite attractive.

An unpublished study carried out by John Logue at the Northeast Ohio Employee Ownership Center (NOEOC) of all companies with ESOPs in Ohio, came up with similar results, if more modest, than those of the NCEO. Logue's study showed an average stock appreciation of 8.9%, three

---

[3] *Employee Benefits in Employee Stock Ownership Plans: How Does the Average Worker Fare?* (Arlington, VA: National Center for Employee Ownership, 1985). Feldman and Rosen used data from two consulting firms about their clients' ESOPs and compared this to the results of their own phone survey in Washington, D.C.-Maryland-Virginia area as a control.

percent below that of the NCEO, and an average annual contribution at 6.2% of payroll, also three percent below the NCEO figure. Using the lower median figures of 8.4% for stock appreciation and 4.7% of payroll for the company contribution, an Ohio employee participating in an ESOP

Table 5.1: Expected value of ESOP stock

Years of Participation	NCEO data	Ohio data	Ohio data for companies where ESOP owns 30+% of stock
1	$1,660	$940	$1,500
2	$3,445	$1,959	$3,183
3	$5,363	$3,064	$5,071
4	$7,425	$4,261	$7,190
5	$9,642	$5,559	$9,567
10	$23,484	$13,879	$26,579
15	$43,357	$26,332	$56,828
20	$71,885	$44,970	$110,615
30	$171,642	$114,623	$376,318

For an employee with annual salary of $20,000.

NCEO - median annual contribution as percent of pay = 8.3%
       - median annual stock appreciation = 7.5%
       - N = 65

Ohio - median annual contribution as percent of pay = 4.7%
       - median annual stock appreciation = 8.4%
       - N = 40

Ohio 30+% - median annual contribution as percent of pay = 7.5%
            - median annual stock appreciation = 12.2%
            - N = 14

Table 5.2: Median family financial assets by age of family head

Age of family head	Total financial assets
Under 25	$ 746
25-34	$ 1,514
35-44	$ 3,750
45-54	$ 4,131
55-64	$ 9,338
65-74	$11,400
75 and over	$10,350

Source: "Survey of Consumer Finances, 1983," *Federal Reserve Bulletin*, September 1984, as cited in Feldman and Rosen.

earning an income of $20,000 a year can expect assets of about $14,000 in 10 years, $45,000 in 20 years, and $115,000 in 30 years. Looking only at companies where employees own at least 30% of the stock, the median contribution rises to 7.5% and the median stock appreciation jumps to 12.2%. Table 5.1 above offers calculations of what an employee can expect to accumulate in an ESOP based on the NCEO data and Logue's study. In order to make a conservative estimate, the medians are used for calculation rather than the averages.

In order to appreciate the impact that such assets will make on the retirement situation of many workers, it is worth noting that the median financial assets of American families where the head of the household is approaching retirement (55-64 years old) is $9,338. Those in retirement (65-74 years old) have $11,400 in financial assets (see table 5.2). These figures can usually be matched by the value of an employee's ESOP stock after only seven or eight years.

While company contributions to the ESOP are current benefits for a vested employee, the employee's taxes are deferred until he or she actually cashes in the stock years later. Furthermore, at that time, taxes can be deferred by rolling the proceeds over into another tax sheltered retirement plan. When the employee does finally pay taxes, it will be during retirement when he or she will presumably be in a lower tax bracket.

Not only does the ESOP provide a worker with a brighter retirement, it also has a significant impact on his or her present attitude about the job. When an ESOP owns a significant portion of a company, a participating employee has good reason to feel more secure about his or her job, resulting in a stronger, long-term commitment.

Job Security and Commitment

It was not too many years ago that the work force in many factories consisted of people whose parents had preceded them and who expected to be followed by their children. Once a worker began working for a company, the future was secure. You could incur a long-term mortgage to buy a home and expect to pay it off. The last two decades have witnessed a bursting of this bubble of simple security. Millions of working men and women have lost their jobs, not due to poor work performance, but for reasons beyond their control: plant relocations, shutdowns caused by attempts to ward off corporate raiders, or liquidation of a company in order to pay the tax on the estate of a deceased owner.

Today's work force is interested in more than just a paycheck. Job security is high on the list of priorities. An employee of a company owned in part or whole by an ESOP can feel that he or she has a degree of control over the future. While employee ownership cannot change the market conditions that may cause hard times, it can change the way a company deals with hard times. Employees have a strong stake in keeping a company afloat. While stockholders can withdraw their capital and reinvest it elsewhere, it is not so easy for a worker to find another job.

In order for management to keep traditional stockholders happy and attract conventional investment capital, it must turn a profit high enough to produce attractive dividends or stock appreciation. While employee stockholders are pleased to receive high dividends and watch the value of their stock increase at a healthy pace, they realize that these are only gravy on the meat and potatoes. The money they have invested through the ESOP is capital invested in their jobs.

ESOP stock is an investment in job security for a number of reasons. The most immediate impact is that it strengthens the company by providing a steady source of new equity capital. ESOP stock also provides a retiring owner with friendly buyers, certain to carry on the business: the workers. This alternative is much more reassuring than a sale to a competitor interested in liquidating the firm and, as a consequence, the jobs. A third way ESOP stock protects workers' jobs is to make it more difficult for a corporate raider to take control of the firm and milk its assets. So even if an employee's stock does not grow as quickly as other investments might, he or she benefits greatly from sustained employment. After all, employee stock is only the source of a secondary income; monthly wages are what primarily put bread on the table.

The partnership between the owner and the employees created by the ESOP not only provides a basis for long term security, but also stimulates a source of employee motivation. "I am always amazed at how sophisticated people become when their self interest is involved," says Lee Morgan of Antioch Publishing. Employees at Webb Insurance Agency ask, "How did *we* do?" "Every year [since the ESOP], we've increased sales and reduced cost of sales," states Jack Hoye of Fluid Regulators.

How does employee ownership motivate employees? There are a number of ways. One way is for the company to pass through dividends to the workers. "There's nothing like pass-through dividends to drive home the virtue of ESOP stock," says Lee Morgan. Even if the dividend is not high, the employee knows that this is a direct fruit of his or her ownership and productivity. Furthermore, the company can now pay these dividends with pre-tax dollars when they are passed through an ESOP.

Second, as the employees acquire a greater percentage of the company through the ESOP trust, they see the relationship between the value of their shares and their own role in the company's success. The average employee at Fluid Regulators, who owns 12 shares, saw the value of his or her ESOP assets increase $5,100 in 1986.

While the appreciation of ESOP stock in some companies may be dramatic enough to catch the participant's eye, employees most often pay attention to the size of their company's annual contribution to the ESOP. As Alan Cohen and Michael Quarrey point out in *Employee Ownership Companies After The Founder Retires* (1985), workers are more likely to respond positively if the company is providing them with a significant financial benefit. "In companies which provide large and sustained contributions to employee ownership plans, employees feel better about their jobs, are more likely to stay with the company longer, and are more interested in the financial performance of the company", write Cohen and Quarrey (p. 10).

While the raw numbers can have quite an impact on an employee's desire to see his or her company grow successfully, there are additional ways that will increase the worker's ability to translate that incentive for success into higher productivity. Many companies, having recognized the positive impact of employee participation in management on productivity, have implemented programs to include their employees in the decision making process. One way is to include workers on the Board of Directors. Antioch Publishing has had two workers on its Board since 1946, long before creating an ESOP.

"We're no longer a dictatorship, we're a democracy," says Glen Webb. At Webb Insurance Agency, the employees make up the Board. Mr. Webb has worked to decentralize decision-making in his attempt "to raise successors." This is especially important in a company where the owner at retirement will leave the entire business in the hands of the employees. Participation on the Board during this time of transition will have a positive impact on the viability of the company under future employee control. Cohen and Quarrey found the efforts of retiring owners to prepare their employees to become future owners had a positive impact on the success of such firms. "The owner thought enough of the employees to make them majority owners in the firm. Also, all of the departing owners selected their successors from among long-term employees, and most of the owners gradually retired as they trained future management" (pp. 10-11).

Cohen and Quarrey found that employee-owned companies outperformed other firms in their industries in increased employment and sales. They felt that not enough research had been done to claim a causal link between the success of these companies and employee ownership. Nevertheless, they were pleased to find that none of the 65 small businesses in their "study became 'sinking ships' after their captains had left" (p. 11).

Not only do many companies include employees in the global decision-making of the Board, some also have formal structures on the shop floor which bring workers into the day-to-day decision-making that can directly affect the conditions of production. Those who are directly involved in production become aware of the little things that cause waste or inefficiency. When they know that there is a link between this waste and the appreciation of their ESOP stock, or the size of their annual dividends, they will *want* to eliminate it. When there is a formal structure of participation which gives them input into the control of the conditions of production, they *will* eliminate it.

The ESOP as an employee benefit is no guarantee that a company will grow. Employee-owned companies have no more control over external market conditions than conventional firms. Nevertheless, when all other factors are the same, the commitment of workers to a company where their ESOP trust owns a significant percent of the stock should be stronger and more long-term than that of the work force of non-employee owned companies. As seen above, firms in Ohio where the employees owned at least 30% of the company enjoyed an annual stock appreciation of 12.2%, 3.8% above the median for the entire group surveyed. The workers of an employee-owned firm have the opportunity to share in their company's growth and capital formation. Their motivation and commitment give their firm an edge in the stiff competition of the market.

6. ESOPS AND YOUR BUSINESS

The greatest expense for many businesses is the cost
of labor. In return for the production of the workers,
an employer pays them wages and benefits. For the most
part, wages and benefits provide an employer with a labor
force and nothing more. Employee Stock Ownership Plans
provide an employer with much more. As is seen above,
ESOPs provide small family business owners with a convenient way to get out of the company at retirement and
to offer their employees a competitive benefits program.
Furthermore, ESOPs are an employee benefit which in addition to motivating employees also improve the financial
situation of a business. Specifically, ESOPs enhance a
company's borrowing power and they increase its available
operating cash. Not only is a business strengthened by
these two factors, employee-owned companies are also in a
better position to avoid hostile takeovers and to maintain
good relations with customers and suppliers.

Taking Your ESOP to the Bank

Few business owners have operated their company for
any number of years without having stepped into a bank
for a loan. Loans provide the entrepreneur with the ability
to expand production when the market grows, or to update
the equipment when competition gets tough. The attrac-
tiveness of an opportunity is directly related to the cost
of the financing needed to take advantage of it. An ESOP
is a handy ally to have when you walk up to the bank loan
officer's desk.

"The banks love us," claims Lee Morgan of Antioch
Publishing, and with good reason. He thinks his company's
access to the industrial revenue bonds in 1985 stems from
the enhanced cash flow that the Antioch Publishing ESOP
provided. Not only do banks respect the strength of a
company with an ESOP, they also are attracted by the tax
benefits of loaning money to an ESOP trust. A bank may
deduct 50% of the interest earned on a loan to an ESOP from

its taxable income. This means that on a $1 million 5 year loan at 8.5% interest repaid in five equal portions, the bank can expect a tax savings of $43,350 (see table 6.1). One can usually expect a lower interest rate from the bank which allows both parties to benefit from the bank's tax savings.

In fact, a survey of banks in Ohio by the Northeast Ohio Employee Ownership Center showed that at least one quarter offered special interest rates to ESOPs averaging 81.6% of prime. The NOEOC study goes on to say that over two thirds of bankers possess some knowledge about ESOPs and over one third favor companies with ESOPs over conventional firms (Bell and Keating, 1987).

A bank loan to an ESOP works in the following way: The ESOP trust borrows money from a bank and the company guarantees the loan. Next, the ESOP trust uses the

Table 6.1: Tax savings for banks on loans to ESOPs			
	Conventional loan	Loan to ESOP	Discounted Loan to ESOP
5 year loan	$1,000,000	$1,000,000	$1,000,000
Interest rate	8.5%	8.5%	7.75%
Interest earned	$255,000	$255,000	$232,500
Taxable portion	$255,000	$127,500	$116,250
Tax rate	34%	34%	34%
Taxes due	$86,700	$43,350	$39,525
After-tax profit on loan	$168,300	$211,650	$192,975
Bank saves	0	$43,350	$24,675
ESOP saves	0	0	$22,500

borrowed money to buy newly issued stock from the company (or the owner's stock in the case of a buyout). This stock is held by the bank as additional collateral which is returned in portions as the ESOP makes payments on the debt. The cash for the debt payments comes from the company profits in the form of tax deductible contributions to the ESOP. *The company not only receives a tax deduction for the interest paid, but also for the repayment of the principal.*

In addition to a likely savings on a lower interest rate, the financial situation of a company with a leveraged ESOP is stronger than that of one with a conventional loan. When a business must make annual loan payments, its net operating earnings must cover payments of interest and principal. *The minimum operating earnings to cover debt service are lower when the loan is through an ESOP* than when it is a conventional loan. In order for a company to pay back a conventional $1,000,000 5 year loan at 8.5% interest, it would need to generate operating earnings of $1,770,150 (see table 6.2). To cover interest and principal payments on the same loan through an ESOP, the company would only have to generate $1,232,500. The difference in net cash flow of $537,650 is due to the fact that the company is repaying the principal in pre-tax dollars with an interest rate discounted to 7.75%. In the first year

Table 6.2: Pretax earnings needed to repay $1 million five year loan -- conventional loan vs. ESOP loan		
	Conventional loan at 8.5%	ESOP loan at 7.75%
Payment of principal before tax	$0	$1,000,000
Payment of interest before tax	$255,000	$232,500
Tax due at 34%	$515,150	$0
Payment of principal after tax	$1,000,000	$0
Required net operating earnings (pre-tax)	$1,770,150	$1,232,500

after the loan, the conventional company would have to show pre-tax earnings of $388,030 as opposed to only $277,500 in an employee-owned company.

In addition to the lower cost of loans through ESOPs, company management will also be pleased with the flexibility of such loans. While some types of financing are tied to capital investments, ESOP loans can be used to buy out a previous stockholder or to buy newly issued stock, providing the business with cash to be used as management sees fit.

ESOPs Shelter Profits for Retained Earnings

The Employee Stock Ownership Plan enables a business to maximize the conversion of pre-tax profits into retained earnings. The corporate tax rate for profits above $75,000 is at 34%. Assume a company, after paying out dividends to its stockholders, wants to retain the remaining $300,000 for reinvestment. If it is organized as a conventional company, it will pay $102,000 in corporate profits tax, leaving only $198,000 to put back into the business. However, if the company were to make a tax deductible contribution of $300,000 to the ESOP trust in newly issued stock, it could retain the $300,000 in cash for company purposes (see table 6.3).

If the company is 100% employee owned, such a move is a simple choice between paying the money to the federal government or retaining it for the employees' future retirement. If the company has less need of the cash, part or all can be passed through the ESOP to the employees as dividends. The ability to pass through dividends also enables the company to shelter profits beyond 25% of payroll. Table 6.4 assumes that the firm chooses to retain two-thirds of the earnings and distribute one-third to employees.

Most companies with ESOPs are not 100% employee owned. In these cases one must take into consideration the position of the other shareholders. The contribution of stock, either from treasury stock or authorized but yet unissued stock, will dilute the *percentage of ownership* of the existing shareholders. However, dilution of the percentage of ownership may or may not have a dilutive effect on the *economic value* of the company. The contribution to the ESOP is, of course, an employee benefit that might otherwise be passed (after taxes) to the existing stockholders. In the long run, however, this is an employee

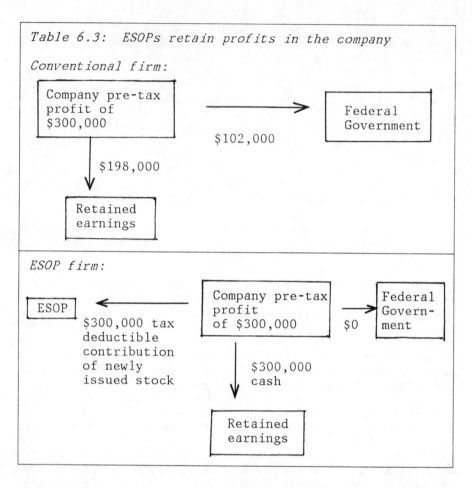

Table 6.3: ESOPs retain profits in the company

Conventional firm:

Company pre-tax profit of $300,000

$102,000

Federal Government

$198,000

Retained earnings

ESOP firm:

ESOP

$300,000 tax deductible contribution of newly issued stock

Company pre-tax profit of $300,000

$0

Federal Government

$300,000 cash

Retained earnings

benefit which not only compensates workers for their skill, dedication and innovation, but also motivates them to higher productivity. This should produce a long term increase in the value of the stock of *all* shareholders -- including both the existing shareholders and the new ESOP owners. Table 6.5[4] illustrates a comparison of a company with and one without an ESOP and the effective "percentage of ownership dilution" and "economic dilution."

---

[4]   Table 6.5 and the related discussion is based on a rough draft by Glenn Laury of Menke & Associates, Inc.

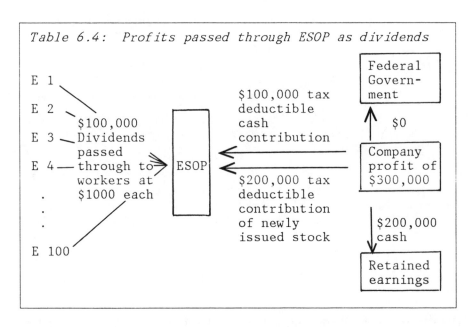

Table 6.4: Profits passed through ESOP as dividends

E 1
E 2
  $100,000
E 3 Dividends
  passed
E 4 — through to → ESOP
  workers at
  $1000 each
.
.
.
E 100

$100,000 tax
deductible
cash
contribution

$200,000 tax
deductible
contribution
of newly
issued stock

Federal
Govern-
ment

$0

Company
profit of
$300,000

$200,000
cash

Retained
earnings

The illustration assumes a typical company with a fair market value determined by five times its earnings which would also equate to roughly twice its stated book value. It also assumes an annual contribution to the ESOP of 4% of a $700,000 payroll. The company without the ESOP would grow at a rate of 4% (roughly the annual inflation rate over the past twenty years). The company with the ESOP would grow at a rate of 7.5% (roughly the annual inflation rate plus the documented average percentage increase in profitability of those companies that had installed ESOPs (Quarrey, 1986).

After eight years the original shareholders would have diluted their percent of ownership by 18.5%. Yet their 81.5% of the company would now have an economic value of $1,352,125 compared to owning 100% of a non-ESOP company with an economic value of $1,315,932. It is clear that if the return on equity is greater than the percentage of ownership dilution, it would make sense to create stock.

ESOPs Strengthen Your Company's Position

No business is an island. All firms must deal with the outside world. Perhaps the most important outside contact is the customer. Regardless of the amount of

Table 6.5: Dilution of ownership and return on equity

Year	% owned	ESOP company Value equity of original owners	ESOP company Net cash flow	Non-ESOP company Value equity of original owners	Non-ESOP company Net cash flow
1	97.2%	$ 972,000	$141,520	$1,000,000	$132,000
2	94.6	1,016,950	151,801	1,040,000	137,280
3	92.1	1,064,331	162,839	1,081,600	142,771
4	89.7	1,114,340	174,692	1,124,864	148,482
5	87.5	1,168,535	187,419	1,169,859	154,421
6	85.4	1,226,027	201,086	1,216,653	160,598
7	83.4	1,287,114	215,762	1,265,319	167,022
8	81.5	1,352,125	231,522	1,315,932	173,703

production, a business can only turn a profit if it can sell what it has produced. Suppliers are a second key group. They affect the cost as well as the consistency of production. A company needs a strong position from which to negotiate for low prices and good service.

The third reality which many firms must deal with is the hostile takeover. When a company does not control the majority of its stock, it is vulnerable to being purchased by an outsider whose interest does not lie in strengthening the business, but in milking its assets. Such actions have been the death blow to many plants and have aggravated seriously the high unemployment in industrial regions such as the Great Lakes area.

Employee Stock Ownership Plans can strengthen a company in dealing with all three of the above realities. They do so by enhancing the longevity of a business and by putting stock in the hands of cooperative investors whose future is linked to the company.

One of the factors that is important to both customers and suppliers is a long-term relationship with a company. Customers want to know that they can count on a firm to provide a needed service for many years. They do not want to be continuously shopping around for new producers. When customers know that they will be dealing with the same firm for a long time, they are confident that they will be treated well. Furthermore, they can plan with more certainty. Customers are willing to pay for what they get and an established company with a strong future is a responsible company worth more, while fly-by-night companies are bargain basement businesses and customers who go to them expect just that, bargain prices.

That the longevity of a business is enhanced by employee ownership is also important to its suppliers. Suppliers are more likely to dedicate their best treatment to companies which are preferred long-term customers. If suppliers are confident that your company will be a source of constant sales for a long time, not only will they provide better service, they will also be willing to offer better prices. As Glen Webb of the Webb Insurance Agency points out in Chapter Three, insurance companies make heavy investments into agencies so that they extend preferred treatment to those which have a means of perpetuating long-term existence. Mr. Webb considers the ESOP an ideal device for perpetuation which has strengthened his agency's position when competing for company contracts.

ESOPs also strengthen a company's ability to resist takeover attempts. One of the biggest risks involved in using the sale of stock to outsiders as a way of obtaining fresh capital is that you do not know who is going to buy it. Previously, if small business owners wanted to keep control of the firm in local hands, they would have to keep enough of their own capital tied up in the business to own more than 50%. When company stock is issued to an ESOP trust, owners are assured that their new business partners share their concern about building the business. Employees have just as many reasons as the previous owners to want the company to continue successfully. Any actions which might be profitable in the short run, but threaten their future employment over the long run, would certainly not meet with their approval. Management can count on the workers to vote with the company to avoid hostile takeovers. And present legislation requires that such decisions be voted on by the ESOP participants.

In short, ESOPs are an example of an employee benefit which returns more to a company than just increased motivation. ESOPs increase a business's credit, they offer a way of augmenting its cash flow, they help build a credible reputation before customers and suppliers, and they provide insurance against unwanted interference from hostile investors.

Is an ESOP right for you?

The previous chapters have elaborated on the many advantages of the ESOP for employee ownership. One disadvantage of ESOPs, relative to other forms of employee ownership, is the cost of establishing them and the annual cost of maintaining them. The tax savings made possible by an ESOP are only an advantage if they are greater than the cost of establishment and the yearly valuation required by law. Cooperatives have no such requirement and are much less expensive to set up initially, too.

The general rule of thumb is that ESOPs are practical only in companies which employ more than 15 employees and have an annual payroll in excess of $250,000. The more profitable the company, the more the ESOP tax saving is worth, provided the payroll is sufficient to cover it.

Establishing an ESOP requires substantial initial costs which include a valuation of the business, legal fees, and initial administration costs. Those costs typically start at $10,000 in setting up an ESOP in a small, closely held business. (The costs can, of course, run higher, and the more complex the deal, the higher the costs.) The annual cost of maintaining an ESOP in a small company typically runs on the order of $2,000 - $5,000 for valuation of the company and $2,000 - $3,000 for administration.

Table 6.6: Covering the cost of your ESOP:
Annual taxable earnings required

(Taxable earnings) > (5 X cost of ESOP)

	No ESOP	ESOP	No ESOP	ESOP
Taxable earnings	$50,000	$50,000	$300,000	$300,000
Cost of ESOP	0	$10,000	0	$10,000
Taxes (Tax rate)	$12,500 (25%)	0	$102,000 (34%)	0
After-tax earnings	$37,500	$40,000	$198,000	$290,000

In order to determine whether the tax savings will be greater than the cost of an ESOP for your business, you must take two factors into account. First, the company's taxable earnings should generally be three times greater than the cost of maintaining the ESOP and the prorated costs of establishing it, for, at the maximum corporate tax rate of 34%, an ESOP can potentially retain for the business only one-third of its profits that otherwise would go for taxes.

Suppose that your ESOP cost $15,000 to establish which you hope to recover over five years and another $7,000 annually to maintain. Thus, to break even on the ESOP, you need to save at least $10,000 annually on your taxes during the first five years. That would require that the firm earn at least $50,000 in taxable income and shelter that in the ESOP in order to break even (see table 6.6). The higher the company profit, the bigger the tax savings can be, provided the company's payroll is sufficient.

The second factor which determines the tax savings value of your ESOP is the size of payroll. The tax deduction available for contributions to an ESOP is limited to 15% of payroll *except* in leveraged ESOPs, where the maximum contribution is 25%. (Interest paid on ESOP loans, which is also tax deductible, is not included in this figure.) This means that even if the company generates sufficient earnings to benefit from a tax shelter, an ESOP may not help if payroll is not sufficiently high. A company with a leveraged ESOP must have a payroll of at least 20 times the cost of maintaining its plan. Assuming an annual cost of $10,000 for maintaining the plan and recovering the initial costs, payroll would have to be at least $200,000. If the ESOP were not leveraged, payroll would have to be $333,000, that is, 33 times the cost. Table 6.7 contrasts the payroll considerations in establishing and maintaining leveraged and non-leveraged ESOPs. Note that net tax savings through an ESOP rise dramatically with payroll and profitability. The ability to pass through dividends since the 1986 legislation would allow companies to shelter beyond 25% of payroll which, in some cases, would make ESOPs feasible with smaller payrolls.

Thus an ESOP can be a money-losing form of employee ownership for a business which (1) has low profits, (2) has a small payroll, or (3) pays too much, relative to profits and payroll, to establish and maintain its plan. In the example above, the company with expected annual taxable earnings of less than $50,000 and an annual payroll under $200,000 (if leveraged) or $333,000 (if unleveraged)

Table 6.7: Covering the cost of your ESOP:
Annual payroll required

Leveraged ESOP:
(annual payroll ÷ 4) > (5 X cost of ESOP)

Non-leveraged ESOP:
(annual payroll ÷ 6.7) > (5 X cost of ESOP)

	Leveraged ESOP	Non-leveraged ESOP	Leveraged ESOP	Non-leveraged ESOP
Payroll	$200,000	$335,000	$2,000,000	$2,000,000
Pre-tax earnings	$50,000	$50,000	$500,000	$300,000
Potential tax savings	$12,500	$12,500	$170,000	$102,000
(Tax rate)	(25%)	(25%)	(34%)	(34%)
Cost of ESOP	$10,000	$10,000	$10,000	$10,000
Net Savings	$2,500	$2,500	$160,000	$92,000

would find that an ESOP costs more than the tax savings are worth.

For the small business in these circumstances which wants to establish some form of employee ownership, setting up a cooperative will probably be more beneficial. While cooperatives do not receive all of the tax benefits of ESOPs, they are eligible for some, including most notably the deferral of taxation on the capital gains when the seller rolls them over into other domestic corporate securities. The start up and maintenance costs are much lower, too.

7. COOPERATIVES AS AN ALTERNATIVE

The previous chapters have elaborated on the many advantages of the ESOP for employee ownership. Still the employees of some firms have chosen to set up a cooperative instead. Often the co-op option is taken because such a structure places a high value on labor and democratic principles. The essential attributes of cooperatives, dating back to 1844 in Great Britain, are that (1) voting on major company issues is based on one person one vote; (2) profits are distributed on the basis of hours worked; and (3) capital takes a subordinate position to labor. In order to qualify for special tax treatment under Subchapter T of the Internal Revenue Code, these principles must be followed (PACE, 1985).

ESOPs are not required to meet these same criteria. In fact, many ESOPs are structured such that the employees act as would shareholders of conventional corporations. Both votes and dividends are distributed according to the percentage of stock owned. Such cases demonstrate that employee ownership and employee participation in management can be mutually exclusive. Naturally, workers seeking to control their business would show an inclination for the cooperative structure.

Nevertheless, employees do not have to forego the numerous tax advantages of ESOPs in order to enjoy the benefits of the cooperative structure. ESOPs too can be structured to create democratically controlled employee-owned businesses. While the Internal Revenue Code sets forth a minimum set of issues which must be voted on by the employees, it does not prevent a company from expanding this set of issues to allow employees maximum control. Furthermore, where state law permits, employees can use such devices as voting pools where they agree to exercise their voting rights on a one-person one-vote basis.

ESOPs can also be structured to parallel the cooperative principle of allocating profits according to labor. There is nothing to deter an ESOP from using a formula which bases the allocation of stock on some measure of hours worked. Dividends would then be paid out on stock

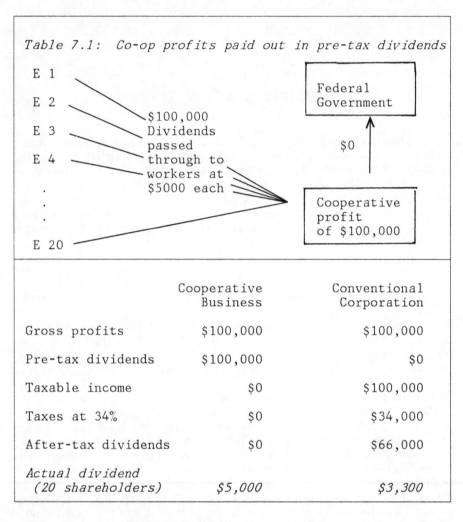

Table 7.1: *Co-op profits paid out in pre-tax dividends*

E 1

E 2

$100,000
Dividends
E 3
passed
through to
E 4
workers at
$5000 each

.

.

.

E 20

Federal
Government

$0

Cooperative
profit
of $100,000

	Cooperative Business	Conventional Corporation
Gross profits	$100,000	$100,000
Pre-tax dividends	$100,000	$0
Taxable income	$0	$100,000
Taxes at 34%	$0	$34,000
After-tax dividends	$0	$66,000
Actual dividend *(20 shareholders)*	*$5,000*	*$3,300*

which is a reflection of the accumulated hours worked. Requiring that employees sell their stock back to the ESOP when they leave the company would ensure that profits, as well as control, remain in the hands of those actively working.

Given the adaptability of ESOPs to a cooperative structure, under most circumstances employee-owned firms would be ill-advised to forego the favorable tax treatment accorded ESOPs. However, the tax savings made possible by an ESOP are only an advantage if they are greater than the cost of the yearly appraisal required by law. The general rule of thumb is that an ESOP makes little financial sense unless the company's annual profit exceeds $50,000 and payroll exceeds $200,000 (These two factors determine an ESOP's tax savings).

If the cost of an ESOP would be greater than the tax savings for your business, you may wish to consider some form of cooperative. The start up and maintenance costs are much lower than those of ESOPs since co-ops are not subject to an annual appraisal requirement. Furthermore, the cooperative structure of employee ownership is still eligible for some important tax benefits. Just as in the case of ESOPs, when you sell your business to your employees as a cooperative, you can postpone paying any tax by rolling over the profit into some other U.S. securities. Furthermore, the new employee owners will benefit from the treatment of dividends as earned income. This avoids the double taxation which occurs in conventional corporations where dividends are paid after corporate taxes have been assessed. The end result is that worker owners receive larger dividends (see table 7.1).

Cooperatives Perpetuate Businesses

While ESOPs have become popular since 1974, the tradition of employee ownership has its roots in industrial cooperatives dating back to the 19th century. Long before Congress legislated tax incentives for the transfer of ownership to employees, workers were joining together to run businesses collectively. Sometimes business owners, attracted to the ideals of economic equality, chose to join with their employees as co-proprietors, without expecting any encouragement from the Internal Revenue Code. Two such people are Sahag and Elizabeth Avedisian, founders of the Cheeseboard in Berkeley, California.[5] In 1967, this married couple opened a retail store specializing in fine domestic and imported cheeses which has grown to be the leading cheese store in the entire San Francisco Bay Area.

---

[5] This account of the Cheeseboard is based on "Paradoxes of Collective Work: A Study of the Cheeseboard, Berkeley, California," by Robert Jackal in **Worker Cooperatives in America** (see Appendix C). Information was brought up to date by a telephone interview with Cheeseboard members in October 1987.

The Cheeseboard markets hundreds of quality cheeses from all over the world, as well as making pizza and sourdough bread, and selling juices and premium foreign beers.

The Avedisians soon found that their business had outgrown their own capacities and found it necessary to hire a few employees. While mostly part-time, these workers were compensated with good wages and benefits. The fair treatment which they received from the Avedisians generated a family atmosphere in the store. Not satisfied with being just a good employer, Sahag Avedisian suggested in 1971 that the six current workers join with him and his wife in repurchasing the business as a collectively owned and run store. Both the owners and the employees took 50 cents per hour wage deductions in order to gather $10,000 over two years which became the purchase price.

The Cheeseboard thrived under collective ownership. By 1975, sales were above $5,000 a week, a 67% increase over 1971. The success made it necessary to move to a new and larger location in 1975 and this in turn stimulated even greater volume, $8,400 per week in 1978. Today, sixteen years since Sahag Avedisian first voiced his interest in sharing ownership with his employees, the Cheeseboard is doing $25,000 of sales per week.

This success is explained by many things. Not least is the excellent relations that Cheeseboard personnel maintain with their customers. A high value is placed on being fair to customers, as well as suppliers. For one thing, the store gives away $20 per day of cheese in taste samples to assure that customers will be satisfied with their purchases. The cooperative atmosphere in the shop also makes it an attractive place to buy cheese and other items. Furthermore, the Cheeseboard cooperative displays concern for its local community by offering discounts of 5% to the self-identified needy and up to 25% for the elderly. Finally, prices are maintained at a low 50% markup compared to 80% or 100% by competitors.

The motivation of the worker-owners is another important factor. In conventional and cooperative businesses alike, wages and benefits are strong incentives for high performance and low turnover. The members of the Cheeseboard cooperative are presently earning $12 an hour. Health insurance is completely paid for those who work more than 20 hours per week, while those working less have 50% paid for by the business. A dental plan is drawn up along the same lines. In 1986, the cooperative also began contributing to a pension fund which is based on the number of hours worked. Over time this will grow to become an important part of retirement for aging members. Meanwhile, worker-owners can borrow from the fund.

The non-traditional characteristics of a cooperative business are also important factors in motivating workers to greater success. The Cheeseboard cooperative now has 23 members. Most work regularly at the store while some only substitute when needed. All members are involved in the operation of the business. Participation takes place at three levels. On a personal level, each oversees his or her own work and is responsible for all decisions which do not affect the other members. In the case of minor decisions affecting others, a proposal is placed on the bulletin board where members can sign their votes or a quick majority vote can be taken at the monthly meeting. In the case of major decisions, a consensus is required at the monthly meeting. No group action is taken if at least one member maintains strong opposition to it. This increases the time spent discussing some difficult questions, but assures full support and speedy implementation in the end.

Given the importance of each and every member, worker-owners gain a sense of control which enhances both freedom and pride. Furthermore, many of the members acquire the confidence that they are capable of starting their own businesses. Employees also learn the value of cooperation, that a willingness to negotiate and take others' perspectives into account can lead to unity and success.

Finally, worker-owners have the peace of mind of job security. Although becoming a member is no easy process, once a member one can rest assured that he or she will have a job for as long as the business continues to operate. New members are selected through acquaintance with existing members. They work a probationary period of 40 hours, during which they interact with every other member. Next, members must decide by consensus to accept the new member. If accepted, the 40 hours of labor are considered the purchase price of membership. If rejected, the hours are paid at the normal rate of pay.

In the case of the Cheeseboard, much of the success is due to the hard work and dedication of the Avedisians to their co-workers. Theirs was a political commitment to the concept of worker-cooperatives. They were not looking for a way to sell their business and retire; rather, they were searching for a form of ownership which fit well with their own values regarding healthy human relations. While the history of co-ops has certainly seen many similar cases, the introduction of favorable tax treatment for small business owners selling to eligible worker-owned cooperatives has expanded interest in co-ops to more traditional business owners. Sharing ownership and control as intensely as in a co-op takes a special kind of person and not every proprietor of a small business would feel comfortable in such a role. In this case, owners will more likely sell a firm to their employees when they are ready to move on to something else or simply retire.

Crumbs Bakery in Athens, Ohio, was sold by the former owner to a group made up of employees and others interested in working there in 1986. The consultant on the project was Worker Owned Network (WON), which has been operating innovative pilot projects to determine whether training in worker-ownership is an effective means of creating and saving jobs for Ohioans.[6]

When Crumbs Bakery owners Steve Koch and Elizabeth Lohrman decided to get out of the business in order to follow some other personal interests, they were still concerned about keeping the five year old bakery in operation. The bakery was in excellent financial shape and the owners were proud of their products and record of growth. Furthermore, they wanted the store to continue to provide jobs for the community.

The bakery proprietors were encouraged by friends of WON to convert the business to a worker-owned enterprise. Through negotiations with WON, an agreement was reached by which a worker-owner group was formed to buy the bakery as a cooperative. A selection committee was formed consisting of one of the former owners, the one employee who was definitely interested in being a part of the new business, a volunteer with experience in hiring and a WON staff person. Selection criteria included entrepreneurial skills, cooperative qualities and a special interest in the bakery business. In addition to the one former employee on the selection committee, the final group of six new owners included two unemployed people and one mentally disabled person who had also worked at Crumbs before.

This group was provided training in ownership, cooperation and management by WON staff. This training as well as legal and technical assistance was made possible

---

[6]   Information about Crumbs Bakery is based on a report written by Worker Owned Network in January 1987.

by an Ohio Bureau of Employment Services grant. Two
months after being selected, the new worker-owners were
operating their business. Mr. Koch and Ms. Lohrman also
worked very closely with the consulting group and new
owners during the conversion period and in the first few
months as job trainers and management consultants in order
to ensure the transfer of skills necessary for the future
success of Crumbs Bakery. Furthermore, the previous
owners were willing to finance half of the purchase price
of the business for the new worker-owners.

The sale of a small, labor-intensive business like
Crumbs Bakery, especially in a small community like Athens, is a difficult task. Not only do the employees provide
a source of prospective buyers, their purchase in the form
of an eligible worker-owned co-op sweetens the sale with
the tax rollover. In the case of Crumbs Bakery, an ESOP
would have been impractical due to the small size of the
business. Yet some employee groups, purchasing a size-
able company where an ESOP would be practical, choose
the cooperative structure anyway. Their decision is most
likely swayed by the traditional belief that co-ops are more
democratic and susceptible to worker control. Franklin
Forge in West Branch, Michigan, is such a case.

Franklin Forge was assisted by the Midwest Employee
Ownership Center (MEOC), a non-profit organization which
provides technical assistance to employees interested in
buying out the original owner. Such centers can provide
sound advice as well as connect the employees with the
necessary resource people. Here are excerpts from a MEOC
summary of the Franklin Forge case prepared by Deborah
Groban Olson and Michael Saggau.

"Unprofitable subsidiaries are often offered for sale
to employees. These situations are very tricky. Employees
must get a feasibility study done by a very skilled consultant, who knows when to say "no" to a bad deal. A
deal like this one was feasible for some unusual reasons.
Both the workers and the management are strong and
skilled. The community needed this plant very badly.
The idea of the buyout came from the workers, not the
corporation. The parent corporation had a compelling
reason to sell at a low price and a public relations reason
to try to make the deal work. So they agreed to a take-
or-pay[7] contract for one year. This contract made it easier

---

[7]   In a take-or-pay contract, a customer agrees to pay

for Franklin to keep old customers and attract new ones, frequently a difficult problem for a new company taking over a facility which has been losing money.

"In early 1984 the employees of Franklin Forge in West Branch, Michigan, became very concerned about the future of their company and the possibility of a plant closing since the forge was losing money. The union, UAW Local 1874, organized a Jobs Committee to investigate what they could do to save their jobs. It functioned as a quality of worklife committee. Upon investigating the financial situation of the company the employees decided that they might best protect themselves by buying the company....

"UAW International Representative Jack Laskowski found assistance for the employees from MEOC and its general counsel. Laskowski also used the resources of the UAW to help the Employee Buyout Association they formed find necessary financing for the feasibility study and the employee buyout....

"In 1984, Harsco wanted to sell or close Franklin.... Harsco was not well placed to close Franklin without a buyer because it had a million dollar take-or-pay contract with the gas utility for at least the following year because it had run a gas line to Franklin. There was no buyer on the horizon as West Branch is not a choice manufacturing location. Thus the employee offer was the most likely offer Harsco would get.

"The employees knew they needed highly qualified management to make a profitable facility out of Franklin, although they also knew it had once been a profitable forge. The entire forging industry is going through a major realignment out of which approximately half the U.S. forging operations will survive. These employees had to find a way to be among that half....

"They contacted a former plant manager of the Franklin plant, Robert Stoner, to be the plant manager. He had managed the plant for Capitol and Harsco for several years and had left after disagreements with the corporation about labor relations and other management decisions. He was well respected by the local business community and local lenders. Bob Stoner was then the chief executive officer of Pacific Forge near Los Angeles. However, he responded to the employees' request to return to run Franklin Forge as an employee owned company be-

---

for a product or service regardless of whether it is used.

cause he felt a strong bond with the employee group and he had a retirement home in the country near West Branch to which he and his wife were quite happy to move.... The employees felt he was fair and knew the forging business. Bob Stoner felt these were some of the hardest working and best forge men with whom he had ever worked.

"It was difficult to raise some of the money needed for this buyout because Franklin had been losing money for the three years prior to the buyout. Union members ... made numerous calls on lenders [and] ... worked very hard to raise funds from the employees and with assistance from International Representative Jack Laskowski to raise funds from various government bodies. The perseverance and positive attitude of the Buyout Association, led by Rich Clark from the UAW and Bob Stoner, with the assistance of this writer, working together, impressed the lenders that this group could make a go of it under employee ownership. Once convinced of this, Bob Beneson, Vice President of the National Bank of Detroit (NBD) Roscommon Bank, became very involved in trying to help find other lenders to participate with his bank in the deal....

"Franklin Forge is a worker cooperative, with ownership of one voting membership share per person and accumulation of equity in internal equity accounts. The membership shares price was initially set at $5,000. Most of the members have purchased their membership shares with loans from the Industrial Cooperative Association (ICA) Revolving Loan Fund or from the Farmers and Merchants Bank of Hale. These loans required a down payment of $250 with payments of one dollar per hour for three years to pay the balance of $4,750. Seven lenders were involved in the buyout financing including the State of Michigan, Ogemaw County, the National Bank of Detroit, the ICA Revolving Loan Fund, the Farmers and Merchants Bank of Hale, the seller and Bob Stoner.

"Franklin Forge increased sales at a much greater rate than expected in its first year. Still, the first year was costly. Franklin expect[ed] to become profitable in 1986. The most spectacular success of the Franklin story is in job creation. At the time the buyout was first contemplated, there were 20 people employed and a seniority list of 82. As of the time of the buyout the management projected that they would have 38 people employed by the end of the first full year of operation. After six months they had 38 employees, and by the end of twelve months 54 were working, and another 15 [were] expected to be coming back to work within the next six months."

Pros and Cons of Workers' Cooperatives

As the three above examples indicate, Employee Stock Ownership Plans are not the only means of setting up an employee-owned business. A workers' cooperative provides an alternative with its own advantages and disadvantages.

The primary advantage of a workers' co-op over an ESOP is the cost. While ESOPs offer many tax advantages not available to a co-op, ESOPs are subject to ERISA laws which cover pension plans and include substantial legal reporting requirements. The cost of this yearly valuation makes them rather expensive. If a business is unlikely to benefit greatly from tax savings, the cooperative may be the appropriate form of employee ownership.

Another factor which often weighs in favor of a workers' co-op is the balance between capital and labor in the business. The value of the stock of a labor intensive business might not hold as much meaning for employees. In such companies, the assets are not likely to increase in value; rather, the motivator is the yearly dividend. In cooperatives, employees are usually paid according to their work, not the value of their holdings in the company.

A third advantage is the simplicity of the ownership. Each worker owns one share of the company. This creates a situation of equality in a very simple way. While equality can be written into the ESOP structure as well, it involves a more complicated process. Workers in a co-op are likely to be aware of their ownership responsibilities. The vote of each has the same weight as that of anyone else so there is no possibility of any minority group taking over.

Despite the advantages mentioned above, there are a number of differences between ESOPs and cooperatives which make the former more attractive. First, participants in an ESOP pay for the company out of future profits with no personal liability. A co-op, on the other hand, begins when each member buys one share by spending his or her own money or taking on a personal debt.

A second difference is that tax benefits available to ESOPs allow both the firm and the employees to defer taxes until ESOP shares are finally distributed; at that time, employees can roll-over the proceeds into a qualified retirement investment. A co-op or its members must pay tax in the year that the dividend is earned. Another ESOP tax advantage that co-ops do not share is the ability to repay loans, such as the original loan to buy the business, with pre-tax dollars.

Co-ops do share some tax advantages with ESOPs. Most significant to an owner is the deferment of taxes on the gain from the sale of at least 30% of his or her business to either an ESOP or a cooperative when the proceeds are rolled over into some other domestic securities. Similarly, an estate may take 50% of the proceeds from the sale of its stock as a tax deduction when it is sold to either an ESOP or a workers' co-op.

Co-ops are at a disadvantage when it comes to attracting outside investment. Since the investor is de-emphasized in favor of labor, co-ops generally must depend on their own members for equity financing. In ESOPs, workers not only do not need equity to obtain stock, their company also has greater access to traditional lending institutions which are attracted by tax incentives.

A fourth difference is that some states have co-op laws which limit the return of the stock per year. ESOPs, on the other hand, have no limit to the return of profits to the employee owners.

Cooperative Options for Retiring Owners

The decision between the use of an ESOP or a co-op structure to convert a conventionally-owned business into an employee-owned firm must take into account the needs and desires of both the workers and the original owner. Under most circumstances, the advantages of the ESOP for the operation of an ongoing company will make this the favored option for both the employees and an original owner who plans to continue with the firm in some capacity. However, as mentioned above, some businesses are simply too small to take advantage of an ESOP.

If an ESOP does not make sense for your business, you still have some flexibility with cooperative structures which will allow you to sell your company and defer taxes by rolling the proceeds over into some other U.S. corporate securities. The *Internal Revenue Code* specifies this tax rollover when the owner of a closely held business sells at least 30% of the company to an ESOP or an *Eligible Worker-Owned Cooperative.* Small business owners who wish to take advantage of this rollover have several options with cooperative structures.

Option 1: Some owners choose to sell their business because they are ready for retirement. They no longer desire an ongoing involvement; they would simply like to get their equity out and transfer it into some more appropriate retirement investments. For these, a one-time sale of the entire business to a cooperative formed by their employees will qualify them for the tax rollover.

Option 2: Other small business owners may be attracted to the concept of being a member of a cooperative. They might choose to join with their employees in forming a co-op. Again, a one-time sale of the business to the co-op would allow the original owner to rollover the proceeds into investments elsewhere while continuing to work in the firm as an equal member. This option is ideal for owners who want to get their equity out and still keep a hand in a business which they spent a lifetime building. For the original owner this would be a form of partial retirement while the other members of the co-op would gain from the continued access to his or her experience.

Option 3: An important advantage of ESOPs for retiring owners is that they are designed to make the transfer of ownership to employees as gradual or sudden as desired. Employees can own anywhere from one half of one percent to 100 percent of the firm. This not only provides flexibility for the original owner, it also gives the employee owners the option of establishing a partnership with non-employee investors. Many business owners prefer this flexibility because it allows them to introduce employee ownership while retaining majority control. At a later date when they are ready to withdraw from the company, the ESOP can buy the remaining portion.

The co-op structure is most easily applied to 100% employee-owned companies. This has led many business owners to believe that in order to take advantage of the tax rollover they must sell the entire business lock, stock and barrel in a one-time sale. This may not be the case.

Apparently, in order to qualify for the rollover the owner need only sell 30% of the business to his or her employees as long as they form an eligible worker-owned cooperative. Such a structure would allow the original owner to retain majority control of the company while offering the workers the opportunity to become owners and cooperatively control 30% of the business. Ideally, this setup would be the basis of a transition period during which the workers could learn the dynamics of cooperative decision making. At a later date, the worker-owned co-op could buy the remaining portion of the business. This

Table 7.2: Eligible Worker-Owned Cooperatives

According to section 1042 (c) (2) of the *Internal Revenue Code,* an Eligible Worker-Owned Cooperative is any organization:

(A) to which part I of Subchapter T applies (any corporation operating on a cooperative basis),

(B) a majority of the membership of which is composed of employees of such organization,

(C) a majority of the voting stock of which is owned by members,

(D) a majority of the board of directors of which is elected by the members on the basis of one person one vote, and

(E) a majority of the allocated earnings and losses of which are allocated to members on the basis of:

(i) patronage
(ii) capital contributions, or
(iii) some combination of (i) and (ii)

option would also reduce the amount of capital needed up front to finance the initial purchase of the firm.

The author is not aware of any businesses which have used this option yet, so if you are attracted to it you will surely need a lawyer and or accountant to investigate the specifics for setting up such a structure which will qualify for the tax rollover. The key element is to be certain that your cooperative is an eligible worker-owned co-op as defined in Table 7.2.

Regardless of the option you choose, and whether you have decided to sell to your employees for tax purposes or out of some personal attraction to workers' cooperatives, the ultimate beneficiaries will be your employees. Steve

Dawson of the Industrial Cooperative Association[8] under-scores that we should not lose sight of this fact.

I believe that four years from now, em-ployee ownership will no longer be just a phrase, it will be a very *old* phrase. No longer will it receive special notice on the evening news, or front-page articles in the business press. Con-gress will have long since tired of granting new tax incentives, and some other financing craze will be the attraction on Wall Street.
Therefore, for employee ownership to sur-vive and prosper without the flattery it will soon lose, we must attend not just to matters of tax legislation and valuation intrigues, we must at-tend to the employee. If employee ownership does not challenge, educate, and give greater dignity to working people, if it means only a few more dollars in the pocket upon retirement, then it will become just another pension plan, and a risky one at that (1986, p. 15).

Employee ownership, whether as a worker-owned co-op or through an ESOP, is only one dimension of bringing your employees into the business. The following chapter expands on the related issue of employee partic-ipation.

---

[8] The ICA, Industrial Cooperative Association, Inc., is a democratically structured consulting organization with 15 staff people. ICA consults for employee-owned companies -- particularly *democratic* employee-owned companies. The ICA has also created a financing arm, the ICA Revolving Loan Fund. The Fund is a $2,000,000 source of risk capital, available exclusively to democratic firms. For eight years now, the ICA and the Revolving Loan Fund have helped create democratic businesses across the country (1986, p. 15).

8. BRINGING YOUR NEW PARTNERS INTO THE BUSINESS

Cost Cutter Stores[9]

"All of us have heard stories about how a retiring owner has sold a business to an ESOP and everyone has lived happily ever after. And sometimes it does work out that way. But not every company can make a smooth transition from a company owned by a single person, group of partners or a family to one owned by its employees. The sellers, for instance, may have been very paternalistic, taking care of everything and everyone. When they leave, employees are on their own and may not be as enthused about entrepreneurship as the seller expects. Or the seller may have run things in a very personal or even authoritarian way, making it difficult to move to the kind of participative culture in which employee ownership thrives. These problems can be intensified if the seller sells out, but remains in a position of some authority in the company.

"As owners, employees may have heightened expectations about their role in the company. At the same time, those in non-owning management positions prior to the ESOP may see the sale to the ESOP as their chance to have more say about running things, now that they are owners as well as managers. Clearly, things will not continue as usual, but just how should they change? Making the transition gracefully can be a difficult process.

"Cost Cutter Stores, a chain of six grocery stores in Washington state, illustrates well both the problems and their resolutions. In 1980, the company had three stores and $14 million in sales. It had grown over the years under founder Robert Hayden's guidance, and now he was ready to cash in his shares. With no heirs to take over, an ESOP looked like an attractive option. The company

---

[9]   This section is reprinted by permission from the National Center for Employee Ownership.

set up a plan and borrowed enough money to buy all his shares. Hayden took back a note to assure the financing.

"Hayden hired Bill Palmer as the new General Manager, but planned to keep an active role in the company. Hayden's expectation, according to Palmer, was that employees would 'appreciate all of this and would be newly motivated to create renewed growth.' But Cost Cutter Stores had always treated employees well, and, according to Palmer, the employees saw the ESOP as just one more benefit among many. Moreover, some were suspicious or skeptical about the complicated plan....

"Part of the problem was that the company was doing well financially at the time, and there was a reluctance to change things. 'Employees were owners,' Palmer noted, 'but we really had not changed the way they were treated.' A halting first step involved group meetings to get people motivated, but these turned into public relations events that accomplished little and were soon terminated. Management then tried a one-on-one approach with employees to obtain ideas and opinions.

"As a result of employee ideas, the company began an aggressive price cutting campaign.... Some items were being priced below cost, and employees began to ask why. 'In all my years in the grocery business, I've never had a box boy question pricing,' Palmer said. But he agreed that the employees had a point, and the prices were raised on some items.

"Changes needed to be made on a symbolic level as well. Palmer had arranged to buy a new car, for instance, but between the time he ordered it and the time it was to be delivered, the company decided it needed to cut costs. Palmer decided to give the car back, even though that cost him money. Driving a new car into the parking lot at that time would hardly be an appropriate symbol, he decided, and symbols now mattered.

"As people began to become more comfortable with these person-to-person changes, more formal mechanisms were set up. Employee and management representatives from each store began a monthly series of Cost Cutter Improvement Committee meetings to discuss ways to improve performance. The most vocal and critical people from each store were purposefully put on the committee by management. By the end of a year, they had become advocates of the process. 'At the beginning,' Palmer said, 'the critics were very tough and just wanted to talk about all the terrible things management was doing to them. By the end of the year, they were urging that more employees in the stores get involved in solving problems.' That advice was heeded, and now there are improvement committees in each store.

"A number of changes have become evident. When things get backed up in one area, such as checkout, employees from other areas get involved. Employees successfully urged the firing of a fellow employee caught trying to take an unearned discount on a turkey, saying that that was stealing from them, and store policy required anyone caught stealing to be fired. Over the last five years, sales have tripled even though the overall market in their area is shrinking. Stock prices have doubled, operating earnings are up and costs are down. Productivity has increased to the point that the Associated Grocers, which measures productivity for its member stores, reports that Cost Cutter scores are 'off its charts,' and even sent people back to remeasure.

"Given this success, it might seem that Cost Cutter has resolved all its problems. In fact, Palmer says some employees remain unenthused, and some stores are still not doing well. Contribution levels to the ESOP are high now because the note to buy the stock is still being repaid, but will be lower in future years. If the stock value does not keep going up significantly, employees may not see regular, substantial increases in their account balances, and Palmer worries that this could cause a decline in motivation....

"Cost Cutter is as good an example as we have found of creative discomfort. In unexpected ways, the ESOP forced the company to consider issues and opportunities it probably would have ignored otherwise. The end results have been beneficial for the employees and the company, but the road there has not been easy."

Ownership Provides the Will, Participation Provides the Way

Studies cited in Appendix E indicate that the performance of employee-owned businesses is frequently superior to that of their conventional counterparts. Employee ownership has been related to higher rates of growth and increased levels of employment. The motor which drives these figures up is productivity. In theory, employee ownership is successful because it motivates workers to higher productivity.

In practice, it is not that simple.

A company's earnings increase either when it produces more or when it reduces the cost of the same level of production. In order for employees to bring about changes in productivity, not only must they be motivated, they must also have the means. As an employee-owner, a worker will see the link between higher productivity and an increase in the value of his or her own stock. This link can stimulate the will to increase productivity; however, without participation, the worker is limited in how much change he or she can cause.

Employees are in direct contact with production. They often perceive weak points that escape their supervisors. Where there are formal structures of participation which seek out the wisdom of the workers, companies have experienced tremendous savings due to the elimination of waste or the implementation of an innovative technique suggested by an employee. This human resource frequently goes untapped under traditional forms of management.

Still, even if there is no formal structure of participation, what is to prevent a worker from pointing out flaws to the supervisor? No one likes to feel inferior to someone else. Yet workers are treated as subordinates to management. When an employee sees an error which falls under the responsibility of the "superior" manager, it is more rewarding to laugh with co-workers about how incompetent management is than to point out the wasteful flaw. But if the wasteful flaw fell within the worker's area of responsibility, then he or she would want to correct it. Participation instills an attitude of responsibility because it allows the worker not only to own stock, but more importantly, to own the process.

Owning the Process: Models of Participation

In many successful employee-owned firms, the employees participate in the decision-making process. Ways of accomplishing this range from structures which resemble conventional corporations to creative new forms of participation tailored to the unique qualities of the firm. Like the financial structure of ESOPs, the participation structures that accompany them can be structured in a variety of ways.

The conventional corporate structure can be modified to allow employee owners to participate in running the company. With full voting rights on the stock held in the

ESOP, employee owners vote on the same issues as traditional shareholders: the election of the Board of Directors, major mergers or the sale of the company. ESOP participants are more knowledgeable than traditional stockholders about running the firm since their jobs provide them with day-to-day contact. Given that employees are better informed shareholders, employee-owned firms could amplify the voting issues to more specific company decisions such as major equipment purchases and large investments.

The privileged knowledge that employees have about their particular jobs, the machines they work with, the tasks they perform daily and their interactions with other employees is an invaluable source of input for good company decisions. This kind of information can be obtained in a haphazard manner through informal communication among employees and supervisors. However, managers usually prefer more systematic methods of obtaining information.

Some firms set up committees and work groups of employees who participate in decisions which directly affect their jobs. Committees deal with such company issues as quality control, personnel issues, and investments. Work groups handle more local concerns. For example, salespeople discuss decisions pertaining to their department.

Decentralizing decision making is possible in employee-owned firms because people are likely to be working toward similar goals. Managers at employee-owned firms find that the implementation of decisions made with employees is much smoother.

Even if most decisions are retained by the Board of Directors, the employees are an invaluable source for evaluating the performance of the Board of Directors. Since employees are directly involved in the implementation of global decisions, they should have a hand in separating the wheat from the chaff. Workers should be involved in the nomination of candidates as well as the actual election.

At Antioch Publishing and Webb Insurance Agency, employees sit on the Board of Directors. Such a situation offers the opportunity to gain immediate input from the workers prior to making decisions. While the membership of employees on the Board has a positive impact on a company, it does not offer the same direct impact on productivity that shop floor participation will provide. The ideal situation is a combination of both.

Whatever the form of employee participation implemented in your business, it will be of great service in avoiding the early difficulties experienced at the Cost

Cutter stores. Employee-owned companies which do not make provisions for formal participation at the outset will find it a useful and necessary element of their success somewhere along the way.

APPENDICES: RESOURCES FOR EMPLOYEE OWNERSHIP

APPENDIX A. EMPLOYEE OWNERSHIP INFORMATION AND ASSISTANCE

Initial Information and Referral

For general information on employee ownership, including recent research results, publications and referrals, contact:

> Midwest Center for Labor Research
> 3411 West Diversey, Suite 13
> Chicago, IL 60647
> (312) 278-5418
>
> National Center for Employee Ownership
> 426 17th Street, Suite 650
> Oakland, CA 94612
> (415) 272-9461

For information on ESOPs, contact:

> The ESOP Association
> 1725 DeSales St. NW
> Washington, D.C. 20036
> (202) 293-2971

For information and assistance on cooperatives, contact:

> Center for Community Economic Development
> Community Service Society of New York
> 105 East 22 Street
> New York, NY 10010
> (212) 254-8900
>
> Center for Community Self-Help
> 413 East Chapel Hill Street
> P.O. Box 3259
> Durham, North Carolina 27705
> (919) 683-3016

Industrial Cooperative Association
58 Day St., Suite 200
Somerville, MA 02144
(617) 629-2700

Philadelphia Association for Cooperative Enterprise
133 South 18th Street, 3rd Floor
Philadelphia, PA 19103
(215) 561-7079

For information on employee ownership in New York, contact:

New York State Center for
Employee Ownership and Participation
53rd Floor
1515 Broadway
New York, NY 10036
(212) 930-0108

For information on employee ownership in Ohio, contact:

Cooperative Work Relations Program
1 President Street
Athens, Ohio 45701
(614) 594-5130

Northeast Ohio Employee Ownership Center
Department of Political Science
Kent State University
Kent, Ohio 44242
(216) 672-3028

For technical information and assistance, particularly in threatened plant closings, contact:

Midwest Employee Ownership Center
2550 West Grand Blvd.
Detroit, MI 48208
(313) 894-1066

State Programs

Since 1979, a number of states have established their own programs to facilitate employee ownership. For more specific information and assistance on state programs, contact:

California - Department of Commerce
Connecticut - Department of Economic Development
Hawaii - Department of Planning and Economic Development
Illinois - Department of Commerce and Community Affairs
Massachusetts - Industrial Service Program
Michigan - Department of Labor
New Hampshire - Community Development Finance Authority
New Jersey - Department of Commerce and Economic Development
New York - Department of Commerce
Oregon - Economic Development Commission
Pennsylvania - Department of Commerce
Washington - Department of Community Development
West Virginia - Governor's Office of Community and Industrial Development
Wisconsin - Council on Economic Adjustment

All states offer a variety of programs that provide technical assistance to businesses. While these programs vary from state to state, the following survey of the existing Ohio programs may give you an idea of what sorts of assistance may be available in your state. For information on your state government's policies, contact the state office that handles business development.

Technical Assistance in Ohio

The Ohio Department of Development (P. O. Box 1001, Columbus, Ohio 43266-0101, (800) 282-1085) provides technical assistance to all businesses -- including those that are employee-owned -- through the following programs:

- Enterprise Zones: Allow property tax abatements for municipalities to attract and keep businesses and jobs in areas where unemployment is high.

- Industrial Development Office: Assists businesses in site selection and provides accurate, up-to-date information on buildings, labor markets, taxes, financing and other data necessary for an informed location decision. The office works in conjunction with the Ohio Economic Development Council, a statewide group of independent development professionals.

- Job Training Partnership: Provides funds to help train economically disadvantaged and unemployed Ohioans for employment opportunities. The federally funded program can provide customized on-the-job training.

- Labor-Management Cooperation: Provides business management and labor with information and resources to adopt successful labor management systems.

- Ohio Data Users Center: Serves as a public information center, providing access to a broad range of census and non-census data including demographic and economic statistics.

- Ohio Industrial Training Program: Assists new and expanding businesses to increase productivity by providing customized training services. The program can fund orientation sessions, training of new and current employees, supervisory training and instructor training and assessment.

- One-Stop Business Permit Center: Responds to individuals interested in starting or expanding a business. The center provides start-up kits and offers assistance in completing state permit and license forms. One-Stop also acts as an ombudsman between beginning businesses and state agencies.

- Ohio Technology Transfer Organization: Provides businesses with direct, one-on-one access to new technology and research through a network of technical and community colleges. The organization works in conjunction with Ohio State University.

- Small Business Enterprise Centers: Provide comprehensive services to small businesses at the local level. The enterprise centers also provide organizational, financial, marketing and technical expertise to small businesses by utilizing local resources.

- Small Business Revitalization Program: Promotes cooperation among state and federal economic development financing programs to maximize the job creation impact of business projects in the state.

- Thomas Alva Edison Partnership Program: Initiates cooperative research and development efforts involving enterprises and educational institutions by providing matching capital.

- Women's Business Resource Program: Assists women interested in starting or expanding a business. The program also works to assure equal access to state assistance programs, in addition to providing direction to other business information sources.

Several Ohio community-based organizations provide assistance to establish employee-owned firms. These operate on a local or regional basis and include:

Common Wealth, Inc.
c o Call On Our People, Inc.
25 W. Rayen Ave.
Youngstown, Ohio 44507
(216) 788-0505

Jobs for People
1216 E. McMillan, Suite 304
Cincinnati, Ohio 45206
(513) 251-9111

Worker-Owned Network
50 S. Court St.
Athens, Ohio 45701
(614) 592-3854

Substantial technical business expertise is available through the Small Business Institute program on a local basis through Ohio colleges and universities. For information on this program and the addresses of nearby participating institutions, contact:

Small Business Administration
1240 East 9th St.
Cleveland, Ohio 44199
(216) 522-4195

Finally, the regional centers for Labor-Management Co-operation, established in 1986, are developing expertise in the area of employee ownership.   For information on this program and the addresses of nearby participating centers, contact:

Office of Labor-Management Cooperation
Ohio Department of Development
P.O. Box 1001
Columbus, Ohio 43266-0101
(800) 282-1085

APPENDIX B. STATE AND FEDERAL
FINANCIAL ASSISTANCE FOR EMPLOYEE BUYOUTS

The principal source of government funding of employee ownership are the ESOP tax breaks described throughout the text. Briefly, these are:

- Contributions of stock or cash, repayment of principal on loans to ESOPs, and dividends paid on ESOP stock are tax deductible (see Chapter Six).

- Taxes on ESOP shares contributed to employees are deferred until distribution of stock, usually at retirement when employees are in lower tax brackets (see Chapter Five).

- 50% of the interest on loans to ESOPs is deductible from the lender's taxable income. The consequence is lower interest rates for borrowers (see Chapter Six).

- Owners who sell at least 30% of closely held companies to employees through either an ESOP or a co-op can defer taxes provided they roll over the gains into other domestic stock within twelve months (see Chapter Four).

- Estates can transfer their tax liabilities to ESOPs or co-ops through providing the ESOP or co-op an equivalent amount of stock. Furthermore, estates selling to ESOPs can exclude 50% of the gain from taxable income (see Chapter Four).

In addition to these tax breaks, employee-owned business can benefit from a variety of state and federal direct assistance programs. While the federal programs are, of course, identical throughout the country, state programs vary widely. In order to give you a sense of the sorts of assistance available, here is a presentation of the federal and state programs currently available in Ohio:

The SBA 504 loan program is available to users with a net worth of less than $6 million, and an after-tax 2-year net profit average under $2 million. This loan is for up to $500,000 or up to 40% of total project cost. The funds can be used for assets with a life greater than 15 years. The interest rate is set at 1% above the long term treasury bond rate. Fixed rates for 10 to 20 years can be arranged. Collateral is a second mortgage with the credit criteria being a cash flow greater than the debt service and appraisal. Total federal funds cannot exceed 50% of the project cost. Must create one job for every $15,000 received. Advantages are greater bank security, rate, and lower down payment; available statewide. For further information, contact the Ohio Statewide Development Corporation at (614) 466-5043.

Industrial Revenue Bonds are available to developers and commercial or industrial users for $10 million and over which can cover 100% of the project cost. Funds must be used for fixed assets or equipment. The rate is 75% of prime, floating or fixed, based on the bank, and is available for terms ranging from 7 to 20 years, matching the life of the asset. The collateral and credit criteria are the same as conventional bank standards. Other allowable sources of funds are conventional equity and or UDAG. The main incentive for using IRBs is the rate; available statewide. Borrowers seeking smaller loans (as low as about $200,000) can take advantage of the Ohio Pooled Bond Program which provides financing for fixed assets at 3/4 of 1% to 3% below market rates for up to 25 years. For further information, contact the Economic Development Financing Division at (614) 466-5420.

The State of Ohio 166 loan program is available to industrial users and developers for a maximum of $1 million or up to 30% of total project cost which can be used for the purchase of real estate, machinery and equipment. The interest rate is fixed at 6% for up to 15 years for real estate and up to 10 years on machinery and equipment. Collateral needed is a first mortgage, a parity first mortgage, or a second mortgage. The credit criteria is based on repayment ability and management capability and calls for a minimum of 25% bank loans and 10% equity as other sources of funds. Must create one job for every $10,000 received. The main advantages for this loan are rate, term, availability and lower down payment; it is available statewide. For further information, contact the Economic Development Financing Division at (614) 466-5420.

The competitive Community Development Block Grant (CDBG) program is available to users or developers through an eligible local government for up to $350,000 per project or community. The local government agency receives the grant and then loans it to the new company. It can be used for fixed assets related to business development and infrastructure. The rate varies with need, ranging from 5% to 7% fixed, and the term is flexible. Collateral needed is a subordinated mortgage based on the project and it is preferred that at least 50% private funding be used. Must create or retain at least five jobs. Incentives for this loan are better bank security, rate, term, availability, and lower down payment; it is available only to small cities (under 50,000 population), villages, townships, and non-urban counties. For more information, contact the Office of Local Government Services at (614) 466-2285.

The Minority Business Development loan program is available to users in business at least one year and at least 51% owned and operated by an Ohio minority resident(s) for $700,000 or up to 40% of total project cost. The funds can be used for real estate, machinery and equipment at a fixed rate of 6%. The term is for 10 years with a 25 year amortization possible. The collateral is negotiable with the credit criteria based on repayment ability. Must create one job for every $10,000 received. The main advantages of this loan are better bank security, term, rate, and availability; this program is available statewide. For further information, contact the Minority Development Financing Commission at (614) 462-7708.

The Urban Development Action Grant (UDAG) program is available to developers and commercial and industrial users. The Department of Housing and Urban Development makes the grant to an eligible local government which then loans it to the company to finance between 15% and 25% of total project costs;

it can be used for fixed assets with a life greater than seven years. It cannot be used for working capital. The rate is flexible and the term parallels the first mortgage. The collateral required is a subordinated first mortgage; the credit criteria is based on project need. Any other source of funds is permitted to be tapped while receiving this loan. The main advantages for this loan are greater bank security and the rate; communities eligible must be from HUD-designated "distressed" areas. For further information and technical assistance, contact the Office of Local Government Services at (614) 466-2285.

Withrow Linked Deposit loans are available to businesses with less than 150 employees. The program provides state compensating deposits to Ohio banks agreeing to make small business loans that create jobs. Funds from this type of loan can be used for fixed assets, working capital, and refinancing debts. The rate is set 3% below present borrowing rate for two years with a possible 2-year extension. The collateral and credit criteria depend on the bank. Any other source of financial aid is permitted with this loan; available statewide. Must create one job for every $15,000 to $25,000 received. For further information, contact the Linked Deposit Coordinator, Office of the Treasurer of State at (614) 466-6546.

The Thomas Edison Program Incubators provide low-cost space and access to business and professional services including legal, accounting, marketing, and financial counseling. It facilitates the start-up and continued growth of new businesses at a low cost. Through state matching grants, rents and fees are at below market rates. For further information, contact Ohio's Thomas Edison Program at (614) 466-5867.

The SBA 7(a) Loan Guarantee is available to manufacturers with less than 250 employees, wholesalers with less than $9.5 million in sales, contractors with less than $2.5 million in sales, and retailers with less than $9.5 million in sales. This is a guarantee on 90% of loans up to $350,000 which can be used for fixed assets, working capital, and start up with 30% equity. The maximum interest rate for less than 7 years is prime + fixed rate 2 1/4%; for more than 7 years, prime + 2 1/4%. The maximum term is 7 years for working capital, 10 years for machinery and equipment, and 25 years for real estate. The collateral required is a general security agreement; the credit criteria are set by the lending institution. The principal attraction of this program is its availability. For further information, contact the Ohio Statewide Development Corporation at (614) 466-5043.

While the SBA 504 and 7(a) programs, the UDAG program, Community Development Block Grants, and Industrial Revenue Bonds are available in all states, the other programs listed above are specific to the state of Ohio. Most other states, however, have similar business assistance programs. For information about what state programs exist in your state, contact the appropriate agencies and departments; the simplest access is through the state information referral number if your state has a central information system.

APPENDIX C. FURTHER READING

Bell, Daniel and Mark Keating. *The Lending Environment for ESOP Companies: The Ohio Bank Study*. Kent, OH: Northeast Ohio Employee Ownership Center (1987).

Berman, Katrina C. "The worker-owned plywood cooperatives." *Workplace Democracy and Social Change*. Boston: Porter Sargent (1982).

Bernstein, Paul. *Workplace Democratization: Its Internal Dynamics*. New Brunswick: Transaction Books (1980).

Bluestone, Barry and Bennett Harrison. *The Deindustrialization of America*. New York: Basic Books, Inc. (1982).

Bradley, Keith and Alan Gelb. "Employee buyouts of troubled companies: Extending ownership to employees has advantages over other forms of restructuring," *Harvard Business Review*, LXIII (1985), 121-130.

Cohen, Alan and Michael Quarrey. *Employee Ownership Companies After the Founder Retires*. Oakland: National Center for Employee Ownership (1985).

Conte, Michael and Arnold Tannenbaum. "Employee ownership: Report to the Economic Development Administration, US Department of Commerce." Ann Arbor: University of Michigan, Institute For Social Research (1978).

Dahl, Robert A. *A Preface to Economic Democracy*. Berkeley, CA: University of California Press (1985).

Dawson, Steve. "Employee Ownership in the 80s," *Building Economic Alternatives*, (Fall, 1986), 10-11, 15.

ESOP Association. *ESOP Report*. Washington, D.C.: ESOP Association. A monthly newsletter.

ESOP Association. *Valuing ESOP Shares*. Washington, D.C.: ESOP Association.

Feldman, Jonathan, and Corey Rosen (1985). *Employee Benefits in Employee Stock Ownership Plans: How Does the Average Worker Fare?* Arlington, VA: National Center for Employee Ownership.

Fusfeld, Daniel R. "Labor-managed and participatory firms: A review article," *Journal of Economic Issues*, XVII (September, 1983), 769-789.

Gunn, Christopher. *Workers' Self-Management in the United States*. Ithaca, NY: Cornell University Press (1984).

Ivancic, Catherine and John Logue. *Employee Ownership and the States: Legislation, Implementation and Models*. Kent, OH: Kent Popular Press (1986).

Jackall, Robert and Henry M. Levin. *Worker Cooperatives in America*. Berkeley: University of California Press (1984).

Jochim, Timothy C. *Employee Stock Ownership and Related Plans*. Westport, CT: Greenwood Press (1982).

Jones, Derek C. and Jan Svejnar. *Participatory and Self Managed Firms*. Lexington, MA: Lexington Books (1982).

Kelso, Louis O. and M. Adler. *The Capitalist Manifesto*. New York: Random House (1958).

Kelso, Louis O. and Patricia Hetter Kelso. *Democracy and Economic Power: Extending the ESOP Revolution*. Cambridge, MA: Ballinger Publishing Company (1986).

Kelso, Louis O. and Patricia Hetter Kelso. *How to Turn Eighty Million Workers into Capitalists on Borrowed Money*. New York: Random House (1967).

Klein, Katherine and Corey Rosen. "Job creating performance of employee owned companies," *Monthly Labor Review* (August 1983), 15-19.

Lindenfeld, Frank and Joyce Rothschild-Whitt, eds. *Workplace Democracy and Social Change.* Boston: Porter Sargent (1982).

Logue, John, ed. *The Ohio Buyout Handbook: A 'How to do it' Guide For Workers Becoming Owners.* Kent, OH: Northeast Ohio Employee Ownership Center (1987).

Logue, John, and Cassandra Rogers. *Employee Stock Ownership Plans in Ohio: Impact on Company Performance and Employment.* Kent, OH: Northeast Ohio Employee Ownership Center (unpublished).

Logue, John, James B. Quilligan and Barbara Weissman. *Buyout! Employee Ownership as an Alternative to Shutdowns: The Ohio Experience.* Kent, OH: Kent Popular Press (1986).

Long, Richard J. "Worker ownership and job attitudes: A field study," *Industrial Relations*, XXI (Spring, 1982), 196-215.

Marsh, T.R. and D.E. McAllister. "ESOP tables: A survey of companies with employee stock ownership plans," *The Journal of Corporation Law*, VI (1981), 551-623.

Midwest Center for Labor Research. "Workers as owners," special issue of *Labor Research Review* (Spring, 1985).

NCEO (National Center for Employee Ownership). *Employee Ownership*, bi-monthly newsletter, provides current information on research, and case studies. Oakland, CA: NCEO.

Olson, Deborah Groban. "Union experiences with worker ownership: Legal and practical issues raised by ESOPs, TRASOPs, stock purchases, and cooperatives," *Wisconsin Law Review*, V (1982), 729-823.

O'Toole, James. "The uneven record of employee ownership," *Harvard Business Review* (November-December, 1979), 185-196.

Pateman, Carole. *Participation and Democratic Theory.* Cambridge, MA: Cambridge University Press (1970).

PACE (Philadelphia Association for Cooperative Enterprise). "Choosing a legal structure for a democratically operated employee owned company: Cooperative or ESOP?" (1985)

Quarrey, Michael (1986). *Employee Ownership and Corporate Performance*. Arlington, VA: National Center for Employee Ownership.

Rosen, Corey (1983). "Employee stock ownership plans: A new way to work," *Business Horizons*, XXVI (September-October), 48-54.

Rosen, Corey and Michael Quarrey. "How Well Is Employee Ownership Working?" *Harvard Business Review*. (September-October 1987), 4-7.

Rosen, Corey and Katherine J. Klein (1983). "Job Creating Performance of Employee-Owned Firms," *Monthly Labor Review*, (August), 15-19.

Rosen, Corey, Katherine J. Klein and Karen M. Young. *Employee Ownership in America: The Equity Solution*. Lexington, MA: Lexington Books (1986).

Rothschild, Joyce and J. Allen Whitt. *The Cooperative Workplace: Potentials and Dilemmas of Organizational Democracy and Participation*. New York: Cambridge University Press (1986).

Stern, Robert and Tove Helland Hammer, "Buying your job: Factors affecting the success or failure of employee acquisition attempts," *Human Relations*, XXXIV (December, 1978), 1101-1117.

Tannenbaum, Arnold, Jack Lohmann, and Harold Cook (1984). *The Relationship of Employee Ownership to the Technological Adaptiveness and Performance of Companies*. Ann Arbor, MI: Institute for Social Research.

Toscano, David J. "Employee ownership and democracy in the workplace." *Social Policy* (May-June, 1981), 16-23.

Toscano, David J. "Toward a typology of employee ownership," *Human Relations*, XXXVI (July, 1983), 581-601.

Trachman, Matthew (1985). *Employee Ownership and Corporate Growth in High-Technology Companies*. Arlington, VA: National Center for Employee Ownership.

Wagner, Ira (1984). *The Performance of Publicly Traded Employee Ownership Companies: Report to the New York Stock Exchange*. Arlington, VA: National Center for Employee Ownership.

Whyte, William F., Tove Helland Hammer, Christopher Meek, Reed Nelson, and Robert Stern. *Worker Participation and Ownership*. Ithaca, NY: Cornell University (1983).

Woodworth, Warner, Christopher Meek, and William F. Whyte. *Industrial Democracy: Strategies for Community Revitalization*. Beverly Hills, CA: Sage (1985).

Zwerdling, Daniel. *Workplace Democracy*. New York: Harper and Row (1980).

APPENDIX D. FILMS ON PLANT CLOSURES AND WORKER OWNERSHIP

The following films can be rented from California Newsreel, 630 Natoma Street, San Francisco, CA 94103, (415) 621-6196, except as otherwise indicated.

Worker Ownership

Blue Collar Capitalism   *film, 1978, color, 30 min*
In April, 1975, Vermont asbestos miners bought their mine when it was to be closed by a conglomerate parent. This film shows key issues that arise when workers become owners. Rental: Cornell University, (607) 256-4405

Buyout   *16 mm color, 1982, 30 min*
This film poses the complex issues surrounding the buyout of an unprofitable GM parts plant in New Jersey by 1,200 workers and managers. Both groups compete to make production and investment decisions, while they also must work together to make the plant profitable.

Collision Course: American Labor and Management at the Crossroads   *45 min*
This 45 minute film examines the development and eventual failure of the worker ownership and participation program at Eastern Airlines.

The Fight Against Black Monday *16mm color, 1978, 75 min*
Describes the efforts of the Mahoning Valley Ecumenical Coalition to develop a plan for keeping the Youngstown Sheet & Tube steel mill open under worker community ownership in 1977.

The Great Weirton Steal　　　*16mm or video, color, 55 min*
A critical view of the Weirton buyout that, in Stanley
Aronowitz's words, "leaves us few illusions that there are
easy answers." Rental: First Fun Features, 153 Waverly
Place, New York, NY 10014 (212) 243-0600.

The Mondragon Experiment　　　*16 mm, 1981, color, 55 min*
Detailed look at the world's largest and most successful
venture in worker-ownership. Located in the Basque re-
gion of Spain, the Mondragon cooperative movement is a
network of 65 enterprises with 15,000 worker members.

Temescaming　　　*16 mm, 1975, color, 64 min*
In Canada, workers and local managers bought their paper
mill from a U.S. corporation to avert closure. Intended
for workers and communities considering employee community ownership.

Plant Closing Problems

Shout Youngstown
A documentary that tells the dramatic story of Youngstown's three plant closings. Steelworkers, their families
and friends describe their efforts to save their jobs and
talk about how the shutdowns have affected their lives.

It's Not Working　　　*16mm color, 1980, 25 min*
Workers from a variety of industries discuss alternatives
to plant closings, such as locally-owned co-operatives to
make their reopened plants economically feasible.

What's Good For GM　　　*16mm color, 1981, 45 min*
Investigates the trade-offs for the community in Detroit
where the Poletown neighborhood was razed to make way
for a new GM factory.

The Reckoning   *16mm color, 1979, 26 min*
Professor Harvey Brenner of Johns Hopkins University
presents fifteen years of research on the effects of unemployment on health.

We've Always Done It This Way   *16mm color, 1979, 36 min*
This film describes the innovative efforts by Stewards at
Lucas Aerospace, a British multinational defense contrac-
tor, to save jobs by developing an Alternative Corporate
Plan.   Stewards developed over 250 new products and
marketing strategies, linking worker skills to existing social needs.

Shutdown   *Videotape*
Rental: UAW

Mad River:
Hard Times in Humboldt County *16mm color, 1982, 54 min*
A rural community in Northern California, critically de-
pendent on the timber industry, seeks alternative economic
solutions to mill closings and an unemployment rate twice
the national average. Rental: Fine Line Productions (201)
891-8240

Business of America   *Video, color, 1982, 45 min*
As basic American industry declines, plant closings are
leading workers and communities to consider buyouts,
worker input into decisions, and other options.   The film
suggests that employees can participate not only in their
daily work situations, but also in economic policy formation.

Labor Management Cooperative Problem-Solving

Jamestown Documentary   *1 2" video, 1975, 60 min*
Examines the efforts of the Area Labor Management Committee in Jamestown, New York, to identify problems and
implement solutions to the decline of local industry.   Rental: Jamestown, NY (716) 661-2262

APPENDIX E. SUMMARY OF STUDIES ON EMPLOYEE OWNERSHIP

- A 1986 National Center for Employee Ownership study by Michael Quarrey found that the most participatory ESOP companies grew 12% per year faster than the least participatory ESOP companies and that *all* ESOP companies in the study grew 46% faster over 10 years than they would have without their ESOPs.

- A 1985-86 study of Ohio firms with ESOPs by John Logue and Cassandra Rogers indicates that almost 40% of them outperformed their industries in job retention and creation; only 4% lagged their industries. Furthermore, the study found that the ESOPs of the most participatory companies had a substantial positive impact on company performance in five out of seven cases, compared to only one in six cases for the least participatory companies.

- A 1985 National Center for Employee Ownership study by Jonathan Feldman and Corey Rosen projected on the basis of a survey of 147 companies with ESOPs that the median employee, who earned $18,000 in 1983, would accumulate ESOP shares worth $30,000 after ten years and $120,000 after twenty years. These figures should be viewed in the perspective that the median family's *total assets* today are about $30,000 and that $120,000 exceeds the total assets of more than eighty percent of American families.

- A 1985 National Center for Employee Ownership study by Matthew Trachman found that companies in the computer and electronics industries that offer ownership to over 50% of the employees had annual sales growth twice as fast and annual employment growth four times as fast as comparable non-employee ownership companies. Companies that offer ownership to only managers, by contrast, had growth rates 50% lower than companies that offer no ownership.

- A 1984 National Center for Employee Ownership study by Ira Wagner of thirteen publicly traded companies that were 10% or more employee owned found that these firms outperformed 62-75% of their competitors, depending on the measure used (net operating margin, return of equity, sales growth, and book value per share). Stock prices in these firms tended to follow industry norms.

- A 1984 study by Arnold Tannenbaum, Jack Lohmann, and Harold Cook of the University of Michigan found that their sample of 115 employee ownership companies performed roughly at the same level as comparable conventional companies during the 1976-1982 study period, but were 10% more likely to stay in business. The authors speculated that the employee-owned firms were more likely to accept lower profits during what were often recessionary years than cut back operations or close.

- A 1983 study by Corey Rosen and Katherine Klein of the National Center for Employee Ownership reported in the August 1983 *Monthly Labor Review* found that companies with a majority of their stock owned by employees generated three times more net new jobs per year than comparable non-employee owned firms.

- A 1980 study by Thomas Marsh and Dale McAllister reported in the Spring 1981 *Journal of Corporation Law* that the annual productivity of ESOP firms increased one and a half percent faster from 1975 to 1979, outperforming their conventional counterparts every year (+.78% per year compared to -.74% per year).

- A study by Michael Conte and Arnold Tannenbaum at the University of Michigan's Survey Research Center found that in a sample of 30 employee ownership companies, profits were 1.5 times as high as those in comparable conventional companies, and that as the percentage of the stock the employees owned grew, the percentage difference became greater.

- Katrina Berman, in a 1967 study done for an IRS court case, found that worker-owned plywood cooperatives were 30% more productive than comparable conventional companies.

APPENDIX F. SUMMARY OF LEGISLATION ON EMPLOYEE OWNERSHIP

- *Regional Rail Reorganization Act of 1973:* This, the first statute to mention ESOPs, required a feasibility study of the use of an ESOP for the reorganization of the Northeast freight rail system into Conrail. Conrail employees ended up owning 15% of the company through an ESOP.

- *Employee Retirement and Income Security Act of 1974 (ERISA):* This law created a specific statutory framework for ESOPs including exemptions from certain requirements applicable to other plans. It provided ESOPs with the unique authority among employee benefit plans to borrow money. It also required ESOPs to invest primarily in employer securities. Since ESOPs were defined as "qualified employee benefit plans," contributions to ESOPs are tax deductible (within limits) and ESOPs must abide by the allocation, vesting, and other rules which ERISA applies to qualified benefit plans.

- *Trade Act of 1974:* This Act created an authority within the Department of Commerce to make certain kinds of assistance available for areas suffering adverse effects from foreign trade. The Act contained provisions providing a preference for assisted firms using ESOPs, but they were never effectively implemented.

- *Tax Reduction Act of 1975:* This Act created the "TRASOP" -- the Tax Reduction Act Stock Ownership Plan. Under it, a company could get an additional 1% credit over and above the 10% Investment Tax Credit if an amount equal to at least 1% of the qualifying investment were contributed to an ESOP meeting the special rules of this act. TRASOPs were phased out in 1981 in favor of PAYSOPs.

- **Tax Reform Act of 1976:**   This Act extended the life of TRASOPs through 1980 and added a provision that allowed the employer an additional 1/2% credit if an employee contribution equal to 1/2% of the qualifying investment were matched by the employer.   The Act contained the unusual Congressional directive to the IRS to rewrite rules it had drafted earlier that Congress considered unfair to ESOPs.

- **Revenue Act of 1978:**   TRASOPs were extended to 1984 (later changed) and rules for TRASOPs were tightened.   The Act also required leveraged ESOPs to offer employees a put option where the stock was not publicly traded.   A full pass-through of voting rights on all allocated shares was made mandatory for publicly-traded companies, while closely-held firms were required to pass-through voting rights on issues which required more than a majority vote.

- **U.S. Railway Association Authorizations of 1979:**   This Act authorized an additional $2 million in loans to the Delaware and Hudson Railroad, provided the company set up an ESOP.

- **Technical Corrections Act of 1979:**   This Act made a number of technical corrections to laws governing TRASOPs.

- **ESOP Improvements Act of 1980:**   This Act further extended the TRASOP credit and made a variety of technical corrections to ESOP law.   The Act also made various technical changes in rules for employee contributions to TRASOPs.

- **Small Business Employee Ownership Act:**   This Act provided statutory authority to the SBA to make loan guarantees to ESOPs and made SBA rules for loans in situations involving employee ownership less restrictive.

- **Chrysler Loan Guarantee Act of 1980:**   As part of the government's loan guarantee to Chrysler, the company was required to set up an ESOP and contribute $162.5 million worth of company stock to it by 1984.

- **Economic Recovery Tax Act of 1981:**   This Act replaced the TRASOP with the PAYSOP -- payroll-based stock ownership plan. Under the PAYSOP, a company could receive a tax credit equal to 1/2% of payroll for contributions to a PAYSOP of at least that amount in 1983 and 1984, increasing to .75% in 1985-7. The Act also raised the limits on how much can be deducted for contributions to a leveraged ESOP to 25% of payroll. Furthermore, the Act allowed companies that are substantially employee-owned to require that departing employees take cash rather than the stock itself when receiving their ESOP distribution. Finally, the Act broadened the put option requirement to include non-leveraged ESOPs.

- *Tax Equity and Fiscal Responsibility Act of 1982:* This Act tightened provisions for all employee benefit plans to reduce abuses. Plans in which 60% of the benefits go to officers, highly compensated employees, and top shareholders, were required to set up faster vesting schedules and follow other rules designed to get more benefits to other employees. New limits were imposed on how much a company can deduct when it has more that one qualified employee benefit plan, and the dollar limit on annual additions to a participant's account was lowered.

- *Trade Adjustment Assistance Act:* This Act reauthorized the program which provided loans, loan guarantees, and technical assistance to firms adversely affected by foreign trade and added amendments providing that preference be given to companies which channel at least 25% of the assistance through as ESOP.

- *Deficit Reduction Act of 1984:* This Act contains significant new tax incentives for employee ownership. They include:

  Allowing the owner of a closely-held business to defer taxation on the gains made by a sale of stock to an ESOP or an eligible worker-owned co-op by reinvesting the gains in some other domestic securities 3 months prior to or 12 months after the sale. Taxes would be due when these latter securities were sold. At the end of the transaction, the ESOP or co-op must own at least 30% of the company.

Allowing commercial lending institutions to deduct 50% of the interest income received from a loan to a company for the purpose of acquiring stock through an ESOP.

Allowing a company with an ESOP to deduct dividends paid directly to ESOP participants.

Allowing an ESOP or co-op to assume the estate tax liability of the estate on a business in return for a stock contribution from the estate worth at least as much as the tax liability.

* *Tax Reform Act of 1986:* While this Act reduced or eliminated many widely used corporate tax benefits, the key tax advantages of ESOPs were retained. Presumably, that will make ESOPs relatively more attractive, although the reduction of the maximum corporate income tax rate from 46% to 34% cuts the value of all deductions. This Act provides for two additional ESOP advantages: an exclusion from estate taxation of 50% of capital gains from sales to ESOPs and co-ops, and the tax deductibility of dividends paid to ESOP accounts and used to repay a loan and of immediate allocations of stock in leveraged ESOPs. The Act also makes mutual funds eligible lenders for the 50% interest income exclusion on loans to ESOPs. Furthermore, it allows excess assets from terminated qualified plans to be rolled over into an ESOP without penalty. The Act generally strengthens the position of employees in ESOPs by reducing vesting periods (from ten to seven years), requiring put options for stock bonus plans, clarifying voting rights, and requiring the distribution of ESOP shares to employees on terminating employment for other reasons than retirement or disability.

INDEX

A

D

Dawson, Steve   74, 92

E

F

H

I

J

K

L

M

R

S

T

V

W